DISPOSSESSING THE WIDOW

Gender Based Violence in Malawi

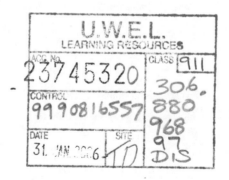

Women and Law in Southern Africa Research and Education Trust

Dispossessing the Widow
Gender Based Violence in Malawi

By Seodi Venekai-Rudo White, Dorothy nyaKaunda Kamanga, Tinyade Kachika, Asiyati Lorraine Chiweza, Flossie Gomile – Chidyaonga

ISBN: 99908-16-55-7
First Published 2002

Kachere Text no. 14

Published by the
Christian Literature Association in Malawi (CLAIM)
P.O. Box 503, Blantyre, MALAWI.

CONTENTS

THE RESEARCH TEAM

The researchers and authors of the book are as follows:

SEODI VENEKAI-RUDO WHITE is the National Coordinator of WLSA-Malawi Office and a lawyer by profession. She holds a Bachelor of Laws Degree from the University of Botswana and a Diploma in NGO Management from the University of London. She is a recipient of the Chevening award and is currently studying for an M.A. in Gender and Development at the Institute of Development Studies at the University of Sussex. Seodi is a gender researcher, trainer and well known activist in Malawi. She was voted 2nd and 3rd place to woman of the year in 2000 and 2001 by the largest circulating newspaper in Malawi, the NATION. Her areas of interest include gender, law, human rights and organisational development.

DOROTHY nyaKAUNDA KAMANGA is a Full Time Research Associate for WLSA-Malawi office and holds a Bachelor of Laws (Honours) Degree from the University of Malawi and a Master of Arts Degree in Women's Studies from the Rutgers University, USA. She is a legal practitioner, researcher, trainer and activist on gender and human rights issues. She is an Africa-America Institute Fellow.

TINYADE KACHIKA is a Legal Programme Officer for WLSA-Malawi. She started as a Part Time Researcher for WLSA-Malawi. Tinyade holds a Bachelor of Laws (Honours) Degree from the University of Malawi – Chancellor College. She is a legal practitioner, gender researcher, trainer and activist.

ASIYATI LORRAINE CHIWEZA is a Lecturer in the Department of Political and Administrative Studies at the University of Malawi (Chancellor College) and a Part-Time Researcher for WLSA-Malawi. She holds a Bachelor of Social Science Degree from the University of Malawi and a Masters Degree in Public Administration from Dalhousie University, Canada. Her research interests include local

4

governance, public sector management and gender issues. Asiyati is a recipient of the Robert MacNamara Fellowship.

FLOSSIE GOMILE–CHIDYAONGA is currently Dean of Postgraduate Studies and Research at the University of Malawi (Polytechnic). She holds a Bachelor of Arts (Honours) Degree from the University of Malawi, a Post-graduate Diploma in Theoretical Linguistics from the University of London and a Master of Sciences Degree in Applied Linguistics from the University of Edinburgh. Flossie is a gender activist, trainer and researcher on women's issues, women and the media as well as language and linguistics. She is also a Hubert Humphrey Fellow.

WLSA would also like to acknowledge the following contributors:

MAGGIE ANTHEA CHIPASULA, a Gender Programme Officer for WLSA-Malawi office.

ZUNZO MITOLE, a Legal Officer at National Bank of Malawi and currently a Part Time Researcher for WLSA-Malawi.

NGEYI KANYONGOLO, a Lecturer in Law at the University of Malawi, Chancellor College.

MATILDA MARCIA KATOPOLA, a senior Programme Officer for the National Democratic Institute, Based in Lilongwe Malawi.

VERONICA KAMANGA, a Programme Officer for a local NGO called Women's Voice.

PREFACE

Dispossessing the Widow: Gender Based Violence in Malawi is a second publication of the WLSA Malawi National Office. The first publication was *In Search of Justice: Women and the Administration of Justice in Malawi* (2000). The book contained results of Stage 1research Phase on Women and the Administration of Justice, Problems and Constraints. It examined the various structures of justice delivery systems and how they impact on women's problems.

Stage 2 of the research Phase whose results are contained in this book, examines how the justice delivery system specifically deals with the problem of dispossession of widows as one of the forms of gender based violence. In order to understand the problem, the book uncovers dynamics as they relate to the nature and cause of the problem. The book reveals how the entire justice delivery system fails to respond to this form of gender-based violence despite the fact that it is a gross violation of human rights.

WLSA Malawi national office has been in operation since February 1998. We are greatly indebted to our WLSA sisters from Botswana, Lesotho, Mozambique, Swaziland, Zambia and Zimbabwe for creating space for us to be part of this regional dynamic set-up. We also recognize the support of the WLSA regional office in Zimbabwe.

This book is written by women from multi-disciplinary backgrounds, working with WLSA on full time and part time basis. Together they were able to make a wide and varied input into the research analysis.

This book uncovers the experiences of the Malawian widow and also of the ordinary Malawian woman. It is a story that helped us grow and realize our own vulnerability and strengths. It is hoped that it will also help other women in that way and will bring change for the better of the Malawian woman.

6

ACKNOWLEDGEMENTS

Women and Law in Southern Africa Research and Educational Trust-Malawi National Office would like to thank the following people and organizations for their enormous contributions in researching and writing this book:

The Danish International Development Agency (DANIDA) for their continued support to WLSA for many years.

The Open Society Initiative for Southern Africa (OSISA) for supporting the Action programme which has contributed largely to this research.

The women to whom this book is dedicated for sharing their stories and experiences with us and therefore enabling WLSA to tell their story to others in the hope of changing the lives of many other Malawian women in a similar predicament.

All the other research participants without whom there would be no story to tell. We thank them for their time, insights and very open discussions.

The regional consultants, Sheelagh Stewart and Naira Khan, for their analytical input into our draft manuscript. This helped us to re-analyse and question some of the issues we took for granted.

Our local consultants, Dr Garton Kamchedzera and Justice Dunstain Mwaungulu without whom the title of the book would not have become what it is. Their tireless efforts in helping us rework the script and the concepts was beyond our expectation. We are further grateful to Mr Edward Chitsulo for his insightful comments on the draft.

The WLSA national and regional sisterhood for showing such a deep sense of commitment and professionalism through long days and nights of research and analysis and good constructive critique of each others work.

7

Agnes Kachiwanda and Kangati Kachere who assisted in typing the report. Our dear families who continue to support us through thick and thin and the many days away from home.

To all people of goodwill who continue to encourage us with the struggle: we say we will not let you down.

Chapter One

INTRODUCTION

Background

In February 1998, Malawi joined the WLSA realm in Phase 4 of "the WLSA" research phase on *Women and the Administration of Justice: Problems and Constraints*. The phase was divided into two stages. During the first stage, WLSA Malawi national office conducted research on the "Justice Delivery System and Its Impact on Women." 'The entry point to justice delivery structures was violence against women. The focus was mainly on the forms of violence that women experience in Malawi and how the justice delivery system responds to such problems. Violence against women, however, was not studied as a substantive issue. The study concentrated on examining and analysing the justice delivery structures that women attempt to access or use when violence has been perpetrated against them.

The study revealed that women access different structures of justice delivery for different forms of violence perpetrated against them. The justice delivery structures include the courts, district commissioners, police, chiefs, churches and *ankhoswe*. Further, the study clearly showed that women experience violence both in the public and private spheres. In both spheres, the forms of violence experienced included rape, common assault, abduction, economic deprivation, dispossession of widows, verbal and psychological abuse. The study showed that one of the most prevalent and entrenched forms of violence women experience in Malawi is dispossession of widows. According to the study, this form of violence is usually downplayed although it causes much psychological, economical and physical harm to women.

This report of the second stage of the above-mentioned research phase takes the study of the justice delivery system further by using dispossession of widows as a case study and as a specific form of violence. The purpose is to examine the perpetration of this form of violence and how the justice delivery system handles such cases. In this context, the Longman *Dictionary of*

9

English Language defines dispossession as taking away possession, occupancy or use from a person.[2] In women's lived realities, dispossession of widows is a process that starts at the celebration of marriage. The process is long and complex and it emanates from an interplay of the construction of gender roles and images, the plurality of legal norms, poverty and cultural factors. It culminates into property dispossession when a husband dies.

The study therefore questions the conventional terminology of "property grabbing" as an all-encompassing concept. As such our approach to the knowledge of this study is expressed to facilitate actions that will contribute to the protection, respect, promotion and fulfillment of the rights of women who survive their husbands.

1.2   Objectives of the Study

To investigate the issue, the study employed a number of objectives as follows:
(i)   To examine and determine the process of dispossession as experienced by widows in their lived realities and its impact on their lives.
(ii)   To examine how women, men and different forms of justice delivery perceive dispossession of widows.
(iii)   To examine the existing relevant laws relating to dispossession of widows, in order to critically analyse the gaps and recommend review.
(iv)   To examine the causes of dispossession of widows in order to uncover the cultural, economic, gender and other dynamics affecting the same.
(v)   To examine individual, community and institutional responses towards matters relating to dispossession of widows and assess how effectively the different structures that deliver justice handle such matters.

1.3   Organisation of the Book

This book presents the findings of the study. Chapter two briefly explains the theoretical underpinnings of the study and the methodology that was used in the investigation. Chapter three conceptualises gender-based violence and property dispossession in order to give meaning to these terms, and determine the scope of behaviours classified as gender based violence and dispossession within the Malawian context. Chapter four discusses the legal context within which dispossession of widows occurs and reveals the gaps and obstacles inherent in the legal system. Chapters five and six present and discuss the findings of the study. These two chapters reveal the gross violation of the human rights of the widow and the inadequate response of the justice delivery system. Chapter seven concludes with a set of recommendations based on the findings.

---

[1] See WLSA Malawi, (2000): *In Search of Justice.*

[2] Longman, (1984): *Dictionary of English Language,* Longman, London.

Chapter Two

THEORETICAL PERSPECTIVES AND METHODOLOGY

Introduction

This chapter discusses theoretical perspectives and methodology that the study uses. The theoretical perspectives and methodology adopted determine issues that are pursued and how the investigation is carried out. The framework of this study draws from a combination of theoretical perspectives and methods in order to get a holistic picture of property dispossession. The problem is examined from various angles in order to gather a full and realistic picture of the constraints women face in society.

2.1 Theoretical Perspectives

Literature review on the issue under study shows that women's use of justice delivery structures to resolve their problems is largely determined by various socio-cultural and economic factors.[1] It is therefore clear that any theoretical perspective used separately would not be adequate to explain dispossession of widows and the response of the justice delivery system. To achieve breadth and depth of analysis, this study employs a combination of sociological and legal theoretical perspectives. The dominant theories the study employs are women's law perspective, gender perspective, social perspective and legal pluralism. The study recognises the contribution each perspective makes to the understanding of dispossession of widows in Malawi. The study, however, does not dwell on detailed theoretical debates on African women and the controversies in various theoretical perspectives. It is an empirical study of real experiences of women in Malawi.

2.1.1 Women's Law Perspective

This perspective recognizes that it is a woman centered legal discipline that enables collection of empirical data about the woman's actual lived experiences and life situations. Its strength is that it is associated with grassroots-

11

oriented methodologies because it records and analyses female life situations and values. It also reveals issues and dynamics that are seldom evident in the male dominated legal culture.[2] The perspective does not regard women as a homogeneous group. It allows an analysis of problems and needs of women with different needs, playing different roles in society and having different socio–economic backgrounds.

One weakness about this perspective is that it introduces a risk of assuming that there are no existing differences. By focusing on women only, it is very easy to assume that the experiences of women are not replicated by men or in the lives of men. It is argued that for a researcher to find out what affects societal attitudes and views and what influences compliance or non-compliance with the law, a deeper understanding of the problem that includes men's perceptions and experiences is needed[3].

It is for this observation that this study seeks to use the Actor Perspective in Women's Law. This perspective does not focus on the woman alone. It is realised that her actions cannot be explained solely by reference to her own character and beliefs. The perspective facilitates research that starts with women's experiences in the process of life management and examines the normative structures and groups that affect her life[4]. It has been argued that the use of the actor perspective adds a dynamic and process oriented dimension to the individual focused women's law perspective. Inheritance research carried out by the Zambia and Zimbabwe WLSA teams shows that individual and communal rights and obligations based on marriage and kinship co-exist in many societies and that these influence the position of women and men and gender relationships[5]. Ncube and Stewart also note that in times of severe economic constraints, individual, communal, customary and statutory rights and obligations create conflicts between men and women, women and women and men and men[6]. Therefore, by focusing on the woman and her relationships with men, other women and the society in which she is embedded, this perspective allows the uncovering of the norms, expectations, social and economic forces which influence dispossession of widows and dispute resolution in Malawi.

To uncover the depth of the widows' lived realities and the extent of the suffering, the study borrows the concept of 'Spirit Injury' from Critical Race Feminist Theory as conceptualised by African American Feminists (CRF)[7]. To the CRF, 'Spirit Injury' refers to the contemplation of the psychological, spiritual and cultural effects of the multiple assaults on women who are victims of gender violence. 'Spirit Injury' leads to the slow death of the psychology, the soul and identity of the individual.

Women come to believe in their own inferiority, and that there is a justification for the violence perpetrated against them because of four main reasons:

12

Firstly, a fundamental part of ourselves and of our dignity is dependent upon the uncontrollable, powerful, external observers who constitute society. Secondly, society places a low value on certain members who in turn perceive themselves as having a lesser worth in that society. Women cannot help but be profoundly silenced and experience a loss of self- actualisation because they are devalued by both the outside society of the oppressor and the inside society of their own culture, as well as by the intimate inside of their own family. Thirdly, spirit injury becomes "as devastating, as costly, and as psychically obliterating as robbery or assault[8]." Finally, this results, on a group level, into the devaluation and destruction of a way of life or of an entire culture.

2.1.2   Gender Perspective
Besides the actor perspective in women's law that might allow inclusion of men as research subjects, this study also makes a conscious decision to include a gender perspective to ensure that data about men's attitudes and experiences in relation to women is collected. Gender as an analytical variable refers to the social construction of male and female roles and relations. It entails, on one hand, men and women's active roles in society and, on the other, ingrained social ideas about what men and women should do and how they ought to behave and interact[9]. Women experience life differently from men due to socialisation patterns that impact on gender differently. Thus gender research and analysis seeks to problematise the relations between men and women. In this study, gender analysis aims to uncover the dynamics of gender differences in dispossession of property in Malawi across a variety of issues. It considers the extent to which men and women are susceptible to dispossession, the perception society holds with regard to ownership of property by men and women. It also considers whether there is any difference in the way men and women respond when they experience property dispossession, and how the family, community and other justice delivery structures respond to cases experienced by men or women.

2.1.3   Social Perspective
Social analysis aims at providing an understanding of women's perceptions and experiences in their own context. The key objectives of the social perspective are to understand the important differences in access, power and perception between social groups, local social organisation and its effects on the issue under study[10]. Social analysis provides information on relevant characteristics of dispossession of widows and vulnerability and social exclusion including the social position of individuals or families distinguished by ethnicity, religion and gender. It further promotes the revelation of the dimensions and effects of social exclusion of various groups such as lack of voice, access to assets, services and community level institutions. The perspective, furthermore, reveals existence and causes of conflicts with-

13

in communities, power and authority as manifested by traditional authority, community leaders and the authority of the state and its agencies, social norms, beliefs, values and institutions such as customary land tenure and common property.

2.1.4   Legal pluralism

Research about women and the law in Southern Africa shows that women's problems are largely resolved at various levels: the family, the administrative system and the courts. The formal law order hence has no monopoly to shape a woman's legal position[11]. Further, it is recognised that research about African women and the law draws on the anthropological approach that employs legal pluralism as a concept to identify situations characterised by the presence, in one social field, of more than one normative order. From this perspective, law is seen as a rule-generating and rule-upholding process occurring in different fora. Thus the term law is broader than the legal centralist's definition[12] and embraces extra legal forces.

The theory of legal pluralism deals with the fact that within any given field, law of various provenances may be operative or when in a social field more than one source of law is observable. It is a situation in which the law and legal institutions are not all subsumable within one system but have their sources in the self-regulatory activities of all social fields present which may support, complement, ignore or frustrate one another[13]. Legal pluralists, according to Tanamaha,[14] insist that the state has no monopoly on law. "There are other normative orders attached to the state which nevertheless are law." These non-state legal orders range from pockets within state legal systems, where indigenous norms and institutions continue to exert social control, to the rule-making and enforcing power of social institutions like corporations and universities. Included are the normative orders that exist within small social groups, from community associations to small football leagues. The family too contains norms for social ordering[15]. This approach to law has been criticised for including the non-legal in the definition of law. The criticism begs the question about who decides what is legal or non-legal? WLSA's previous research on Women and Administration of Justice showed that a majority of Malawian women use the non-legal forms of normative ordering[16]. The Malawi research team recognises the pluralistic nature of law despite the criticisms levelled against legal pluralism.

This study therefore uses the legal pluralism perspective to understand how norms and expectations generated in the intersection between customary law, statute law and people's practices inform the position of women and gender relationships and dispossession of widows. The idea is to obtain a holistic picture of the factors affecting women's lived realities and the choices they make, and decisions that are forced upon them.

14

2.2   Methodology

This section describes how the study was carried out. It starts with a discussion of the study areas and the rationale behind the choice of each area, followed by a discussion of sampling and sample size. Finally, the data collection methods are discussed.

2.2.1   Study Areas

The study on property dispossession in Malawi proceeded on the premise that social-cultural and economic dynamics prevailing in a given locality are essential to the understanding of the subject in question. The choice of study districts, therefore, was based on the perceived social cultural differences in these societies. A purposive decision was therefore taken to choose areas that are matrilineal and those that are patrilineal. In addition, the study regarded regional differences so that the sampled areas represented the three regions of the country: Southern, Central and Northern.

2.2.1.1 Matrilineal Societies

Research in matrilineal societies was undertaken in the following areas: Blantyre, Mangochi, Mulanje and Dedza districts

Mangochi District is in the Southern Region of Malawi with a population of 610,239[17]. Its population is predominantly Yao. However, there are people of other ethnic origins such as the Chewa, Tonga and the Tumbuka, particularly along the lakeshore. The research was undertaken in the town area, in Traditional Authority Jalasi and Malindi areas. In terms of literacy, Mangochi is one of the country's districts with low literacy rates. According to the 1998 census, 23,233 females as compared to 36,643 males are able read and write Chichewa and English. This aspect was found to be an important factor in this study because it has a bearing on issues of civic awareness concerning inheritance laws and other legal procedures.

Mulanje District was chosen because it is one of the highly populated districts in Malawi. It has a land area covering 2,056km^2 and a population of 428,322. This district was chosen for the study mainly because it has two distinct ethnic groups: the Lomwe and Yao. It was thought interesting to study the dynamics of two ethnic groupings living side by side. The research was undertaken in the areas of Traditional Authority Nthilamanja and Namputu Village and in the central district area. In terms of literacy status, 35,797 females are able to read and write Chichewa and English as compared to 50,632 males.

Blantyre District is the commercial hub of Malawi. Like similar cities in the country, Blantyre District is urban, peri-urban and the rural. The research

15

was undertaken in the peri-urban settings of Traditional Authority Machinjiri and the rural setting of Lunzu in Traditional Authority Kapeni's area. Urban area data collection mainly focused on the justice delivery structures. In rural and peri-urban areas, the research conducted general group discussions with women and men. Blantyre, because of its commercial setting, has a heterogeneous population of 809,397. In terms of literacy status, 126,484 females are able to read and write Chichewa and English as compared to 168,056 males.

Dedza district is in the Central Region of Malawi with a population of 486,682. Men are a lot more literate than women are, with the figures of 38,928 and 26,987, respectively. Dedza is predominantly Chewa. Research was undertaken in Traditional Authority Chinyamula area.

2.2.1.2 Patrilineal Societies
Research in the patrilineal societies was undertaken in the following districts: Chikwawa, Mzimba and Nkhata Bay.

In Chikwawa, in the Southern Region, Lunkhwe Village was the patrilineal society chosen. Chikwawa is a home to Senas and Mang'anjas. Chikwawa has a total population of 356,682,where 36,289 men are able to read and write English and Chichewa as compared to15,300 women.

In Mzimba, the patrilineal village chosen was Enukweni Village. Mzimba is home to Tumbuka and Ngoni ethnicities. According to the 1998 population census, Mzimba District has a total population of 610,994. In Mzimba, 12,172 males are able to read and write English and Chichewa as compared to 10,595 females. Nkhata Bay is occupied by the Tonga and has a population of 164,761. In Nkhata Bay 2,318 men are able to read and write English and Chichewa as compared to 2,108 women.

In terms of economic activity status, in all the districts visited, most men and women are engaged in small-scale farming and trading activities. Some households in Mangochi rely on small-scale fishing as a chief source of income. In Blantyre, formal employment in the main city provides an additional source of income for some, mostly men.

In terms of judicial structures, all the districts have magistrate courts. In the case of Blantyre, it is also the site of the Principal Registry of the High Court and the Malawi Supreme Court of Appeal. Lilongwe and Mzimba, too, have district registries of the High Court. The government maintains an administrative system at the district level. The system's offices include social welfare offices and district assemblies. Villages are organized under customary law with authority vested in a village headman who reports to the group village headman who in turn reports to the traditional authority. The Office of the President under the Chiefs Act supervises the traditional authority.

2.1.2   Sampling and Sample Size

Within each district, villages were chosen in consultation with the district assembly offices and the traditional authority of the area. The determining factor was the ethnic groupings present within a particular village. Care was taken to ensure variety of ethnic groupings across the villages to allow comparative analysis.

Within the villages/areas, individual widows and widowers were identified through a sampling method known as 'Dung Beetle Method'[18]. This method involves finding out from members of the local population those who have experienced the problem under investigation. The method was chosen because there are no formal records of widows and widowers in the country. The advantage of using this method is that it enables an in-depth investigation of how a problem manifests in specific circumstances and the various ways in which the family, community and other institutions address it. The major disadvantage is that it is difficult to show the extent of a problem or prove that a problem exists because the choice of number of units is an iterative process and is difficult to be determined in advance.

In this study, the use of this method entailed certain activities in each research site. The research started with a general community meeting of men and women on the issue of property dispossession and its various dynamics. The aim was to gain a better understanding of the research site. These meetings were also used to find out men and women whose spouses had died so that they could be isolated for individual in-depth interviews. Records from various justice delivery structures were also used to find out widows and widowers who had their property dispossessed. The numbers that were found were limited to the number of people who turned up for such community meetings or those that were actually recorded or could be remembered by the institution in question. Those identified were isolated for individual in-depth interviews. The numbers, therefore, varied from district to district.

2.1.3   Data Collection Methods

The study mainly used participatory assessment techniques to provide deeper insight into the issue of property dispossession and discovering what influences women's decisions to seek justice from different structures to resolve the disputes. Participatory assessment is an interactive research process that seeks to understand issues from the perspective of a range of

17

stakeholders and to involve them directly in planning follow-up action[19]. Thus, the techniques enabled women, community members and other stakeholders to define the dynamics of property dispossession in a particular area among particular ethnic groups. However, the woman's perspective was central in this study. Apart from extracting information from the women and other stakeholders, the methods were also used as tools for empowerment where information was immediately given back to the communities on areas of need. The research combined four data collection methods.

2.1.3.1 Group Discussion Method

Group discussions were conducted with men and women separately and with mixed groups. The purpose was to gain an overview of people's practices within an area, the dynamics of property dispossession and the people's perceptions of how individuals, the community and the existing justice delivery system respond to such cases.

2.1.3.2 In-depth Individual Interviews

In-depth interviews were used to collect data generally from women and men and from widows and widowers. The aim was to target individuals whose spouses had died and elicit information on how and why property dispossession occurred or never occurred. Both men and women were carefully targeted to elicit information about different circumstances of victims.

2.1.3.3 Key Informant Interviews

Key informants were people approached for their views and knowledge of property dispossession issues in the various villages and districts. In this regard, views and opinions were solicited from diverse individuals such as village headmen, traditional authorities, counselors, district commissioners, magistrates and court clerks, social welfare officers, ordinary women and men. The value of this method is that it enables validation or refinement of the data collected through the group discussions.

2.1.3.4 Secondary Sources

The research also used information and statistics already available before the research exercise began. It included perusal of research reports from other countries, government reports, books, journals, court cases and records kept by various justice delivery structures. These sources were reviewed to analyse the dynamics of property dispossession and how people resolve disputes in practical and responsive ways beyond the walls of the formal court.

Data Analysis

As a qualitative study, the data was also analysed qualitatively. The whole research process was treated as an integrated interactive process from topic selection to the final write up of the report. Analysis started right in the field where researchers discussed major issues that were emerging from the research and their implications on property dispossession. After the field-work, the research team had a workshop to discuss and gain consensus on key issues coming out of the interviews and how individual data analysis had to be approached. Each researcher then wrote up a preliminary data analysis report based on field interviews, discussions and observations. Each researcher's report was circulated and all researchers had a chance to read and critique one another's preliminary report.

After this reading several meetings followed where the reports were discussed, the data was scrutinised further until the researchers came up with clear categories that the data was fitting into. These discussions and meetings enabled the team to come up with chapters and the contents of each chapter. This also led to a review of the title of the study itself. Thereafter, responsibility for writing each chapter was assigned. The chapters were discussed, critiqued, re-arranged and re-written several times until a rough draft was produced for editing internally and externally.

Conclusion

The theoretical perspectives and data collection methods the study adopted were preferred because of their potential to elicit property dispossession information in a holistic manner. The theories and methods therefore determined necessary strategies to answer the research objectives, what has been revealed through this investigation, and the generation of appropriate recommendations.

---

[1] See Ncube, W. and Stewart J. (ed.) (1995)

[2] Bentzon *et. al*, p98.

[3] Ibid, p94

[4] Bentzon *et. al*. p101.

[5] Ibid.
[6] Ncube, W. and Stewart J. (ed.)

[7] For a good discussion of the critical Race Feminist theory see Wing, A (1997)

[8] Ibid.

[9] Bentzon, *et. al*. p83.

[10] Department for International Development, Sustainable Livelihoods Guidance Sheets, p3.

[11] This position has been documented in a number of studies. See Bentzon et A. W. *et al*, (1998): p31; WLSA Malawi, op.cit.

[12] Bentzon *et al* say legal centralism starts from the standpoint that state law or state recognised and enforced law is the most important normative order and all other norm creating and enforcing social fields are either illegal insignificant or irrelevant.

[13] Griffith, J. (1986): Number 24, p39.

[14] Tanamaha, B. Z, (1993): "The Folly of the Social Scientific Concept of Legal Pluralism" in *Journal of Law and Society*, Volume 20:3, p193.

[15] Ibid.

[16] See WLSA Malawi, op cit.

[17] All population figures in this document are from *The 1998 Malawi Population and Housing Census Report* by National Statistical Office,Zomba, Malawi. December, 2000.

[18] For a good discussion of this method see Bentzon *et al*, p 164.

[19] Department for International Development, Sustainable Livelihoods Guidance Sheets, p8.

Chapter Three

CONCEPTUALISING GENDER VIOLENCE AND PROPERTY DISPOSSESSION

3.1 Introduction

Gillian Walker stresses the need to pull together the conceptual processes underlying the whole debate of violence against women. She argues that, "[The] process of making the experience of oppression in our homes visible to ourselves and getting it accepted as a matter of public concern was one that involves defining it as an issue or problem in our own terms."[1] Walker describes the conceptualisation process as one occurring over time and dictated by activities and events. It is not a mere abstract linguistic concern. She argues that when operating in this 'technical way', concepts are not simply descriptive linguistic conventions. They organize the social construction of knowledge, ways of thinking about, defining, and giving abstract and generalised meaning to our particular experience. Knowledge thus produced provides for particular ways of taking action. Concepts, therefore, do more than name a phenomenon. They are part of a social relation that creates and organises particular phenomena in specific ways, providing responses to what has been identified. Tang *et al.* contend that any study on violence against women should attempt to define the concept because it is through naming that a certain object, event or feeling comes into existence.[2]

How Violence Against Women is defined and conceptualised, whether narrowly or broadly defined, affects a variety of issues. Defining violence against women includes determining the scope of behaviours classified as violence against women, the public perception of the seriousness of the problem, the kind of research to be done, the mobilisation of social resources and the formulation of policies to curb the problem. To determine whether property dispossession is a form of violence, this study conceptualise gender violence, before examining property dispossession in its socio-legal context.

21

3.2 Defining Gender Violence

Gender violence involves unequal power relations between men and women. Most often, men are the perpetrators and women the victims. Gender violence includes but is not limited to physical, sexual and psychological harm (including intimidation, suffering, coercion and /or deprivation of liberty within the family or within the general community and also includes that perpetrated by the state.)[3] Gender-based violence inhibits a woman's ability to enjoy rights on an equal basis with men. The focus of the study therefore is mainly on violence which is perpetrated against women, hence, violence against women.

Various international instruments define violence against women. The Declaration on the Elimination of Violence Against Women states under Article 2 read together with Article 1 that violence against women constitutes "threats of acts, coercion or arbitrary deprivations of liberty to women, whether occurring in public or private life"[4]. Further, the declaration states that violence against women:

> "[E]ncompasses but is not limited to: physical, sexual and psychological violence occurring in the family and in the community, including battering, sexual abuse of female children, dowry-related violence, marital rape, female genital mutilation and other traditional practices harmful to women, non-spousal violence, violence related to exploitation, sexual harassment and intimidation at work, in educational institutions and elsewhere, trafficking in women, forced prostitution and violence perpetrated or condoned by the state."

The UNFPA gender group defines gender-based violence in the same way as the Declaration on the Elimination of Violence Against Women but adds that it is derived from unequal power relations between men and women and that it includes intimidation.

The above definitions seem to be all-embracing and can accommodate all forms of violence against women and their causes and manifestations. However, what constitutes physical, economic and psychological violence differs from one community to another. Organisations and authors, therefore, give various definitions reflecting different areas of emphasis. Some authors advance a narrow definition. In this regard, Alemiki states that "acts of violence refer to physical attack or aggression against a family member by another. The attack must be intentional, and aimed at intimidating or frightening the target or inflicting injury or pain on the victim"[5] Alemiki therefore restricts violence to physical acts of violence amongst family members. Though narrower, his definition is useful as physical aggression amongst family members still needs to be investigated. Roxanna Carillo has defined violence against women as a function of socially constructed norms of acceptable behaviour that can only be reduced and eliminated through fundamental changes in the status of women and attitudes towards men and women in society.[6] Carillo's definition differs from other definitions. It provides a guide on measures to eliminate violence against women through the changing of the status accorded to women. The definition is very relevant. It regards acts of violence as a function of socially constructed norms of acceptable behaviour, as property dispossession is. However, for WLSA Malawi violence against women includes a function of socially constructed norms of unacceptable behaviour.

In Malawi violence against women has been tabled at national level. The Government of Malawi's National Platform for Action follow-up to the 4th World Conference on Women identifies violence against women as one of its priority areas. Being an action follow-up, the National Platform is a powerful agenda for the empowerment of women. According to this document, violence against women refers to:

> " [A]ny act of gender-based violence that results in sexual, or psychological harm or suffering to women, including threats to such acts, coercion or arbitrary deprivation of liberty, whether occurring in public or private life. It is a result of unequal power relations between men and women, which prevents women from full advancement and enjoyment of their freedoms."[7]

Analyzing this definition, any act that results in harm, psychological or physical, is an act of violence.

On a more grounded note, a study into women's access into the justice delivery system in Malawi uncovered a local definition of violence against women.[8] This study used violence as an entry point. The term violence was literally translated as *nkhanza*,(meaning harshness) in Chichewa, the predominant local language in Malawi. Asked what *nkhanza* was, women and other key informants included in their perception acts of property dispossesion, battery, abuse, financial and physical neglect by their spouses.

Violence against women is translated and understood by government, nongovernmental organizations, civil society, members of parliament as well as women's rights activists in Malawi as *"Nkhanza kwa Amayi"*. This phrase currently defines previously culturally condoned negative behaviours against women occurring in private and public.

Nkhanza, so translated, encompasses acts of physical as well as emotional abuse. This agrees with the above definitions, and in particular those provided in the Beijing Platform for Action and the Declaration on the Elimination of All of Forms of Violence against Women as articulated earlier. Further, this understanding complements the definition that Heise offers.

She defines violence against women as including "any act of force or coercion that gravely jeopardizes life, body, psychological integrity or freedom of women in service or perpetuating male power and control." Included here would be rape, battery, femicide, genital mutilation, incest, psychological abuse, sexual harassment and property dispossession.[9]

In conclusion, violence against women should indeed be viewed as a form of gender-based violence directed at women because of their gender. Violence, therefore, is an engine for the maintenance of unequal power relations between men and women in society. Therefore our understanding of violence cannot be limited to either the personal sphere of family relationships, or to a man/woman relationship. Neither can it be limited only to the physical aspect. It extends beyond the physical to include emotional, psychological and sexual abuse. Violence must be seen as a reflection of deeper socio-economic processes which are patriarchal in nature.[10]

3.3 Property Dispossession as Gender-Based Violence

Property dispossession takes many forms. These include grabbing, seizing, diverting or disposing of deceased property. Of these, property grabbing is the most widely used term and is sometimes used to entail all forms of property dispossession. There are however problems with the term "property grabbing" because it is an incorrect term to use to define the taking of property from widows. The term is andocentric because the act is perpetrated against women because they are women. It is a term for circumventing the act of theft since the grabbers take what does not belong to them against the property rights of the widow. The term also fails to describe the aspects of violence that occur when property is taken from the widow. Admittedly property dispossession is commonly done through physical removal of objects of property. The injury perpetrated against the widow transcends physical injury and in some it is hidden because of socio-legal norms and the vulnerability of women. To this end the term "property dispossession" is adopted to adequately bring out the meaning given to the act.

Property dispossession is one of the most notable acts of gender-based violence, which has become prevalent in Malawi and in many African countries. It is taking possession of, seizing, grabbing, diverting or disposal of deceased property thus causing deprivation or any harm to a person entitled under a will or on intestacy.[11] Since it is normally widows who are entitled to property under a will or on intestacy that suffer when deceased property is taken from them, it follows that property dispossession is gender-based violence.

Property dispossession is usually undermined as a form of violence. This is because there is purportedly a confusion and misunderstanding of the term

24

'violence against women.' There is a tendency to separate issues of physical violence from other violence. For example, issues of property dispossession are often not viewed as violence[12] although they may injure the woman economically, emotionally, spiritually and even physically.

In the context of the WLSA Malawi study, the phrase "property dispossession" is in relation to the permanent taking of property from a spouse and/or children of a deceased spouse upon his or her death. The property need not necessarily form part of the estate of deceased. In many cases the property is taken away without considering that it may not have formed part of the estate of the deceased spouse or that some of it may belong to the surviving spouse. This arises out of the wrongful assumption on the part of the dispossessors that, at death, all property is transformed into deceased spouse's estate. More importantly, the taking is not in compliance with legal procedures. Legally, only a lawfully appointed administrator or executor has the authority to deal with property forming part of the estate of a deceased person. However, the taking that constitutes property dispossession is done without such lawful authority. Owen confirms this observation by saying,

> "[T]he problem is so severe in Malawi.... In practice as soon as the husband dies the relatives of the man descend upon his home and forcibly help themselves to any of his assets on the pretext that they are his rightful heirs. By the time the provisions of the Act have to be applied to the estate, substantial diversion of property will have occurred to the detriment of the widow and children."[13]

The victim of property dispossession is more often a widow. It is assumed that by reason of her sex, she could never have contributed to the acquisition of the matrimonial assets and therefore her deceased spouse's relations should have primary control over the estate or access to its benefits. However, the fact that such assumptions are even made in situations where the widow herself is economically empowered, the conclusion tends to lead to the fact that the taking away of the property is sometimes done as a manifestation of domination by the male side over the widow. In some situations the persons taking the property do not even need it. There, it is obvious that the intention is just to dominate over and injure the feelings of the widow as a surviving a spouse.

Property dispossession is primarily a form of psychological and economic violence. It is psychological in that it gives rise to psychological problems like anxiety, depression and fear. It is economic abuse in so far as the practice changes the lifestyle of the victim, sometimes to a situation where she cannot even make ends meet. Sometimes, property dispossession may even include an element of physical violence when the act is accompanied by the actual use of force.

3.4 The Concept of Poverty and its Feminisation

To the extent that property dispossession is a form of violence against women, it relegates the victim of property dispossession to poverty. Also the existence of plural legal systems in Malawi has meant that women are victims of property dispossession. Culture also perpetrates property dispossession by insisting that the woman (whose property has been taken away from her) should persevere in silence. All these factors have led to the relegation of women into poverty hence the feminisation of poverty.

The meaning of property dispossession is therefore further amplified by the contexts within which the acts are perpetrated. In the Malawi context, three factors are significant: poverty, legal pluralism and culture.

3.4.1 Poverty

It has been said that poverty is not just lack of what is necessary for material well-being. Rather, poverty manifests itself in what people are being deprived of in the lives they lead. Therefore poverty has been defined as the denial of opportunities and choices most basic to human life. In the case of the issue of property dispossession therefore, the task would be to consider the choices and opportunities that widows, as opposed to widowers, are deprived of as a measure of feminization of poverty. These opportunities could be the opportunity to lead a long, healthy and creative life, to enjoy a decent standard of living, freedom, dignity, self-esteem and respect from others. Human poverty is multi-dimensional. As such, deprivations in some dimensions can be explained by other factors and not merely by low incomes. For example, a person with a low income may not necessarily be excluded from social life. She may still enjoy good health and be able to lead a creative life. But if she is deprived of some opportunities, she will still be deemed to be in a state of poverty even if she does not have a low income.

As such, in measuring feminisation of poverty, we are encouraged to focus on choices and opportunities that people are deprived of rather than focussing on income earnings only. *The Human Development Report*[14] introduced a non-income-based measure of human poverty, which is also multi-dimensional. This is the Human Poverty Index (HPI). The HPI focuses on four key dimensions: survival, knowledge, decent standard of living and social participation.

For an engendered understanding of human poverty therefore, the question should be, what restrictions do women face on their choices and opportunities that men do not? The answer to this question reveals that such gender restrictions lead to lower incomes for women as well as important choices and opportunities.

26

Poverty has also been defined in relative and absolute terms as well as quantitative. It is therefore necessary to consider what is meant by poverty in all these terms within the context of the WLSA study in Malawi. In relative terms, poverty is associated with a state of deprivation or disadvantage in relation to a given standard of living. Examples of definitions that capture this perception entail "inability to attain a minimal standard of living". Poverty has also been defined as a state of want, disadvantage and deprivation. However, within different contexts, 'the minimal standard of living,' 'the state of want' and 'disadvantage' mean totally different things. For example, in India poverty is viewed in a wider sense. It is associated with lack of incomes and assets, physical weakness, isolation, vulnerability and powerlessness.[15] In Malawi the condition of poverty is characterised by lack of productive means to attain basic needs such as food, water, shelter, education and health. It encompasses all those who are unable to meet nutritional requirements and essential non-food needs equivalent to $40 per capita per annum.[16] In absolute terms, poverty is associated with starvation and hunger.[17] Sen argues that starvation and hunger are the absolute core of poverty. In relative terms, poverty is therefore mainly measured in terms of low-income levels.

This discussion clearly highlights one important aspect that needs to be considered in any poverty analysis: quantitative measures such as income or consumption need to be supplemented with qualitative measures. Therefore within the context of this study, poverty is being looked at from both quantitative and qualitative angles. While focusing on the issue of incomes and how they affect women's access to justice, the study also focuses on the vulnerability of women as an aspect of poverty. Specifically, the focus is on how property dispossession is an aspect of poverty and what constraints it places on the livelihood initiatives of women.

In Malawi poverty is largely feminised. One major recent change in family household structure which has attracted much comment has been the rise in the proportion of households headed by women.[18] The reasons for this increase are diverse for different countries but it is generally evident that the number of female-headed households is related to marriage strategies, property and inheritance issues. Of particular interest in this study is female headship and poverty because it is central to the issue of feminisation of poverty. While it is generally agreed that women are the primary victims of poverty, female-headed households are among the core poor. In Malawi where most female headed households are divorced, widowed or single, opportunities for female headed households to engage in self-employment and productive work are limited due to competing demands on their time in terms of child care, household tasks, and their main responsibility as the main economic providers.

With regard to poverty this study focuses on the extent to which a widow enjoys the basic opportunities and choices after the death of a spouse. According to the HPI, these are the opportunity to lead a long, healthy and creative life, to enjoy a decent standard of living, dignity, freedom, self-esteem and respect from others. Also added to these is the right to enjoy property accumulated during a marriage. In contrast to all these choices and opportunities, widowers usually have the freedom to remarry, to associate with others, to carry out economic activity, to enjoy property accumulated during marriage while such opportunities are limited for widows. Widowers also, in contrast to widows, have high self-esteem, they have many opportunities, maintain a decent standard of living and lead a creative life.

3.5 Widowhood and the Plurality of Laws and Systems

The widow exists in a plurality of legal systems. These systems, as institutions, also directly or indirectly contribute to her dispossession. The context of the perpetrators of property dispossession therefore transcends family members and the private. Dispossessors operate in both the private and the public spheres of life. As such, a useful concept of property dispossession is not limited to the private/public divide. The perpetrators include specific individuals, systems, organizations and courts. The individuals, organizations and courts together construct widowhood and enhance the widow's vulnerability so that she can be economically exploited. In this regard, the links between property dispossession, widowhood, poverty and legal pluralism constitute a synergy of causes for the poor enjoyment of the rights of women who are widowed. Amidst such synergy of causes, the widow's choices for redress and her opportunities to demand the enjoyment of her rights are severely reduced or curtailed. Since human rights are interdependent and indivisible, the lack of enjoyment of her property and other economic rights adversely affect the widow's other rights. Consequently, the widow's vulnerability as a woman is exerberated, her dignity, participation survival and development are either compromised or deprived from her.

3.6 The Cultural Context

As well as the plurality of legal systems the widow is also exposed to various cultural aspects that determine how she prevents or responds to the problem of property dispossession. In some cases, culture demands that the widow should be the vulnerable mourner. In addition culture demands that she should remain silent and refrain from asserting her rights. Cultural norms may also condone the perpetration of property dispossession. This research hence considers cultural aspects attached to property dispossession for a holistic exposition of the problem.

Conclusion

Property dispossession against widows is a form of violence against women which threatens the enjoyment of women's rights. The dispossession of the widow itself is a long and complex process emanating from an interplay of the construction of gender roles and images, the plurality of legal norms, poverty and cultural factors. The solution to this problem may lie in such laws, institutions, cultural factors, gender equality and justice. However, perceptions and actions pertaining to these factors have to be examined from a feminist perspective. In this regard, the study questions certain conventional terminology such as property grabbing as an all encompassing concept. As such our approach to the knowledge in this study is expressed to facilitate actions that will contribute to the protection, respect, promotion and fulfillment of the rights of women who survive their husbands.

[1] Walker, G. (1990)

[2] Tang C. s. *et al* (2000)

[3] Malawi Human Rights Resource Centre, 1999): workshop paper. From women in Development to Gender and Development

[4] Article 1

[5] Alemiki, E.,

[6] Cited in Elliot, F.R. 1996

[7] UNICEF/GOM, (1997) AT P.35

[8] WLSA Malawi,2000

[9] Heise, Lori 1990

[10] Aarchakl Kapir," Nov.1998

[11] Section 84A, Penal Code, Laws of Malawi.

[12] Sakala, F.(1998) p. 30

[13] Owen,M. 1996

[14] *UNDP Human Development Reports*

[15] Chambers R. (ed)

[16] United nations / Government of Malawi , Situation Analysis of Poverty in Malawi 1993

[17] Sen, 1981 Development Practice and Violence against women in Gender and Development.

[18] Sen, 1981, Supra

Chapter Four

THE LAW AND THE DISPOSSESSION OF WIDOWS

4.1   Introduction

This chapter discusses the relevant law on the dispossession of widows. It also discusses the existing judicial structures regarding the application and enforcement of the law of succession and inheritance and, in particular, how the complex issue of property dispossession is dealt with in the Malawian context. It also makes a critical analysis as to what extent Malawian jurisprudence has evolved with regard to the law of succession and inheritance. In turn, the analysis, coupled with the research findings, provides the direction which legal and institutional reforms should take. The relevant law stems from international law, domestic statutes and the common law.

4.2 Applicability of International Law to Malawi Law

International law contains minimum standards to evaluate local standards in their adherence to human rights. In this regard the bedrock instruments are the Universal Declaration of Human Rights (UDHR)[1], the International Convention on Civil and Political Rights, the International Convention on Economic and Social Rights and the Convention on the Elimination of All Forms of Discrimination Against Women.

International legal standards are particularly important in Malawi because the Constitution[2] encourages courts, where applicable, to have regard to current norms of public international law and comparable foreign case law in interpreting the principles of the constitution. More explicitly, the Constitution provides that any international agreement ratified by an Act of Parliament forms part of the law of the Republic if so provided for in the Act ratifying the agreement.[3] Further, international agreements entered into before the commencement of the Constitution form part of the law of the Republic, unless parliament subsequently provides otherwise or the agreement otherwise lapses.[4]

Though international law has been recognised as part of our law,[5] it cannot easily be applied as its incorporation depends on a ratifying Act of Parliament.[6] This provision has been criticised as limiting the applicability of international law in Malawi.[7] The limitation is unjustifiable in the light of the Vienna Convention on Applicability of International Human Rights Law in Domestic Law[8]. The Convention provides, among other issues, that a party to a treaty may not invoke provisions of its internal law for failure to honour an international obligation.[9]

The Constitution provides that customary international law, unless inconsistent with the Constitution, or an Act of Parliament shall have continued application. This provision clearly flouts the spirit of the Vienna Convention as it makes international law subject to the provisions of national law.[10] The starting point for Malawi has therefore been recognised as the need to localise international law in the country's own legislation.[11] However, it has been recognised that the Constitution leaves room for the operation of international law either through courts' decisions, compliance with international obligations or already existing international law binding before the 1994 Constitution.[12]

The judiciary and other organs of the government can therefore take advantage of these accommodating provisions to implement the state's obligations under international law. In this regard, the courts need to use international instruments that enshrine the rights of women.

Specific Human Rights Instruments and their Impact on the Rights of Women in Malawi

Malawi is under an obligation to realise the right to equality between the two sexes. International law further recognizes every person's right to acquire, own and dispose of one's own property. Malawi has a duty therefore under international law to eliminate dispossession of widows.

4.3.1 The Universal Declaration of Human Rights[13]

This declaration is one of the roots of special rights for women. It stipulates that:
- all human beings are born free and equal in dignity and rights.[14]
- both men and women are entitled, without any discrimination, to equal protection by the law.[15]

31

- everyone has the right to own property alone and/or in association with others.
- no one should be arbitrarily deprived of his property.[16]
- everyone has a right to a standard of living and right to security in the event of … widowhood.[17]

The Universal Declaration of Human Rights was intended to be non-binding and was meant to state mere aspirations of nation states. However, the document has become part of binding international law. First, the standards as laid out in the declaration were re-enacted into two covenants which are binding on States. These covenants are the International Covenant on Economic and Social Rights (ICESR)[18] and the International Covenant on Political and Civil Rights (ICPCR)[19]. Secondly, the Malawi Supreme Court of Appeal has held that the declaration applies and is enforceable in Malawi.[20] The Court went further to say that the Universal Declaration on Human Rights is part of Malawi's law and the freedoms which that declaration guarantees must be respected and can be enforced in the courts of Malawi. Therefore, it is clear that where inequality exists, Malawi has to put steps to end the inequality. Further, the said inequality may not be used as a basis for infringement of the right to own and dispose of property and the right to security upon becoming a widow.

4.3.2 The Women's Convention on the Elimination of All Forms of Discrimination Against Women[21]

The Women's Convention is a landmark international legal document in the recognition of women's human rights and their equal status with men. In consideration of section 211 of the Malawi Constitution, it is part of Malawi law as the country ratified it before 1994. The Women's Convention notes that despite the existence of various international instruments promoting equality of rights of men and women, extensive discrimination against women continues to exist.

The Women's Convention requires nation states to do the following:
- Ensure through the law and other appropriate means the practical realisation of the principle of the equality of men and women.
- Establish legal protection of rights of women on equal basis with men and to ensure, through competent national tribunals and other public institutions the effective protection of women against any act of discrimination. [22]
- To take all appropriate measures, including legislation, to modify or abolish existing laws, regulations, customs and practices which constitute discrimination against women.[23]
- To give women equal rights to conclude contracts and to administer

property. In this regard women are recognised as having the right to own, acquire, manage, administer, enjoy and dispose of property whether free of charge or for valuable consideration.[24]

General Recommendation 21 of the Committe on CEDAW condemns discrimination with regards to the division of property based on the premise that the man alone is responsible for acquiring and disposing of the same. The recommendation states that contributions of non-financial nature ought to be accorded the same weight as financial contributions.[25]

4.3.3   The African Charter on Human and People's Rights

At the regional level, Malawi is a party to the African Charter on Human and People's Rights which emphasise that men and women have human rights that must be protected by the state.

The African Charter specifically provides for the elimination of every form of discrimination against women and also ensures the protection of the rights of women and children.[26] The Charter recognises the need to highlight the issue of non-discrimination of women and children. It further encompasses all conventions and declarations which protect women and children. This is a unique feature of the African Charter as it binds all member states of the OAU to all international documents dealing with women and children[27].

4.3.4   The SADC Declaration on Gender and Development

As a member of SADC, Malawi has signed the SADC Declaration on Gender and Development. This declaration recognises, *inter alia*, that gender equality is a fundamental right and that discrimination against women continues to exist. It also commits SADC member states to repeal and reform all laws, amend constitutions and change social practices which still subject women to discrimination. It therefore urges governments to protect and promote the rights of women and to prevent and deal with the increasing levels of violence against women and children. Further, an addendum to the declaration: the Prevention and Eradication of Violence Against Women and children recognises that violence against women and children reflects unequal power relations between men and women, and results in the domination and discrimination against women by men.

This addendum commits the government to take measures to ensure elimination of violence in the legal, cultural, socio-economic and political spheres. States are under obligation to provide services, education, training and awareness as well as budgetary allocations for the elimination of violence against women and children.

Recognising, therefore, that the act of dispossessing the widow is a form of violence against women, government, through its various branches, has the duty to ensure that violence is eliminated by implementing its obligations under all these instruments.

4.4 Domestic Law and its Impact on Women's Rights

4.4.1 The Constitution of the Republic of Malawi

Malawi's Constitution was enacted in 1994. It creates at least three sources of duties to eliminate property dispossession of the widow. First, in chapter three, the principles of national policy oblige the state to actively promote the welfare and development of the people of Malawi through the adoption and implementation of policies and legislation aimed at, *inter alia,* gender equality. To realise this, the state is required to consider and implement principles of equality, non-discrimination and policies to address social injustice such as domestic violence, insecurity of the person, economic exploitation and the infringement of rights to property. Secondly, under chapter four, the equality clause prohibits discrimination on the basis of sex.

Women are recognised by the Constitution as having equal rights with men. In its regard women have equal capacity with men to enter into contracts, to acquire and maintain rights in property, acquire and retain custody, guardianship and care of children and have an equal right in the making of decisions that affect their upbringing. Further, every woman has the right to citizenship and nationality. Other rights pertaining to the woman relate to a fair disposition of property held jointly with husband and a to fair maintenance upon divorce. To protect these rights, the Constitution outlaws discrimination on the basis of gender or marital status and calls for legislation to eliminate customs and practices that discriminate against women, such as violence and, in particular, deprivation of property.

WLSA recognises that in as much as the Constitution highlights the rights of women, it falls short of expounding on certain rights especially as they relate to rights to property in marriage, which issue forms the core of this study. Section 324 recognizes the right to a fair disposition of property held *jointly* with a husband. In this regard, the constitution only recognizes jointly held property and not property *commonly* held in marriage. This poses difficulties since women, generally due to socio-economic construction, do not ordinarily have purchasing power. Purchasing power is a source of joint ownership.

Women generally contribute effectively to the well being of the family through reproductive and productive labour. This must be recognized to create entitlement to the matrimonial property in pursuant to General

34

Recommendation 21 of the committee on CEDAW. Eventually this entitlement of property can be translated into equitable distribution of property upon the death of a spouse. The oversight by the Malawi Constitution is therefore unfortunate. This is further compounded by the fact that our law does not regulate the ongoing family with its focus on inception and end of marriage. The result is uncertainty over the issue of ownership of property upon the death of one spouse. In the case of widows, this can result in the dispossession of the widows. In this regard dispossession therefore starts at the time a woman enters into a contractual relationship of marriage because the law fails to protect the woman in respect of her inherent right to own property.

Thirdly, the constitution pinpoints how the courts may interpret its provisions. It requires the judiciary to use principles of public international law in its interpretation[28] and comparable foreign case law. Through this, the trend to eliminate property dispossession of widows and gender-based violence in Malawi can be applied in Malawi. Bearing in mind the limitations of the constitution as stated earlier, there is need to harmonise this provision and that of Section 211 as discussed earlier.

An answer to this would be to examine the preamble of the Constitution and the principles of national policy set out in Chapter III. These two indicate that the spirit of the Constitution supports to a very large extent principles of gender equality set out internationally and/or otherwise.

4.4.2 The Wills and Inheritance Act
The Wills and Inheritance Act deals with the inheritance to and administration of estates of deceased persons. This Act is important as it determines property distribution intestate and intestate succession matters. The distribution of property under a will (testate) is usually straightforward under Malawian law. This is because the Act provides for testamentary freedom whereby the testator or testatrix is free to distribute property according to her or his wishes. Distribution would then follow the wishes of the testator.[29] The problematic area is intestate succession. Dispossession of property in the Malawi situation occurs both in testate and intestate succession. It is however more pronounced in intestate succession. In any case the majority of Malawians die intestate. This section will proceed to highlight the provisions for the distribution of the property of a deceased man or woman.

4.4.2.1 Distribution of the Estate of a Male Intestate
The Act [30] exhaustively makes provision for the distribution of property that belongs to a male person who has died without leaving a will, but is survived by a wife, issue or dependant. However, a similar positionis not made in respect of the estate of a deceased woman.

The Wills and Inheritance Act provides that if the deceased man's marriage was arranged in the patrilineal system[31], half share of his estate must be distributed amongst his wife, children and dependants. His heirs at customary law acquire the remaining half share.[32] If the marriage of the deceased man was arranged in the matrilineal system, his wife, children and dependants must acquire $^2/_5$ share of the estate. Heirs in accordance with customary law are entitled to the remaining $^3/_5$ share.[33] Under the Act, districts which fall under the matrilineal system include all the districts in the central and southern regions of the country, except for Nsanje and Chikwawa.

While the Act defines the words issue, child or dependant[34], those who are to be entitled as heirs at customary law are not defined.
Section 2 (1) defines the terms as follows:

Issue: in relation to any persons means the children, grandchildren and more remote descendants of that person.

Child: includes an illegitimate child, an adopted child and a child who is not yet born (child *en ventre sa mere)* and grandchild.

Dependant: in relation to a deceased person means a person who was maintained by that deceased person prior to his death and who was:
- a child, issue, wife, parent or *mtsibweni* (uncle) of that deceased person; or any other person living with that deceased person; or
- a minor whose education was being provided for by the deceased and who is incapable wholly or in part of maintaining himself or herself.

The Act does define a customary heir or state that these will be defined according to a specific customary law. Therefore, it is difficult to determine on the face of it what a customary heir is unless a court of law declares a customary heir under a particular customary law. Such lack of clarity allows illegal claimants to stake claims and disposses the widow if their designated share is deemed insufficient.

4.4.2.2 Principles for the Distribution of the Property
When the share that should be jointly inherited by the widow, issue and dependants is ascertained, there are legal principles that govern its distribution amongst them.[35] This may be the $^1/_2$ or $^2/_5$ share, depending on the marriage and custom of the district in which the deceased man's marriage was arranged.

The law[36] provides that before any prescribed share is distributed amongst the widow, issue and dependants, provision should first be made for the dependants. This indicates that the estate cannot be distributed to the wife and children of the deceased person in their own right until provision is made for all dependants which includes themselves. The Act uses the words *distribution* and *provision* which in our opinion provide for two distinct separate meanings. Arguably, *provision* is only meant to offer protection against 'hardship' while *distribution* is the 'actual sharing of the estate amongst beneficiaries.

Thus under the Act, the intention is first to protect all dependants from hardship. Such protection is afforded by ensuring that the dependants are provided with the ordinary necessities of life according to the way of living that they enjoyed during the lifetime of the deceased person. In any event, such protection should be offered in so far as the property available for distribution can provide such protection. In the case of a minor, it includes provision of the opportunities of education he or she could have expected had the deceased person lived. [37]

After ascertaining that such protection has been achieved, the remaining property, except for household property, can be divided between the widow(s) and children of the deceased person.[38] It should be noted that under the law, household belongings such as furniture, beddings, crockery, cooking utensils, garden and farming equipment including other articles used in and for the purpose of maintaining a dwelling house[39] automatically vests in the widow and can not therefore be distributed as part of an estate of a deceased person.[40]

4.4.2.3 An Examination of Property Distribution Principles
The mode of distribution under the Act lacks responsiveness to the interests of the widows and the enjoyment of their property rights. The following problems highlight this argument.

i. Dual Inheritance Capacity of Some Dependents
The wording of the law embraces the customary values that there cannot be one heir to the estate of a deceased person. The whole family is eligible to inherit. As such, the mode is more favourable to the members of the extended family, at the expense of the widow. A problem emanates from the fact that the widow's right to inheritance is measured at the same level with the rights of other dependants. Under the Act, 'dependants' can include almost all the kinsmen/women.[41] A widow enjoys no special inheritance rights as a surviving spouse.

Consequently, the widow may end up being the minor beneficiary of her own husband's estate. With the major beneficiaries being the other dependants, who may also inherit as heirs at customary law. So while the rest of the dependants may enjoy dual inheritance capacity, the widow only has a fraction of the half or $^3/_5$ share. This disregards a widow's entitlement to the matrimonial property and only reduces her to the position of dependent. Further, the relegation of a widow to 'dependent' is degrading to her specifically and to women in general. It connotes that women are generally dependents in a matrimonial household as opposed to persons with rights and capable of acquiring, disposing and sharing property.

ii. Unreasonable Protection Accorded to Some Dependants

The second problem relates to the yardstick that is set by the law in making the provision for dependants. The law aims at achieving protection from *hardship* by providing each dependant with the type of basic necessities that such a dependant was enjoying during the lifetime of the deceased person. In any event, the dependants would be protected from hardship, in so far as the property available for distribution can provide such protection. In the case of a minor, then provision has to be made for the opportunities of education he or she would have expected from the deceased person.[42] The problem is that this yardstick is not achievable in the light of the definition given to dependants. The definition of dependants is too wide and all-encompassing and thus makes it difficult in practical terms for dependants to be so protected as was intended by the law. Even if they were to be adequately protected, a large part of the estate would be consumed in the process, leaving the widow with no sufficient inheritance in her own right.

iii. Ambiguity Over Widows' Property Rights

The third problem is that the Act seems to encourage the prevailing assumption that once a husband dies, all matrimonial property transforms into his estate. While the law on intestacy states that "intestacy shall only be in respect of the property to which the deceased person was entitled to at the date of his death,"[43] in practice, this spirit is quickly lost. Further, the law does not emphasize the fact that it is just 'part' of the matrimonial property that can be subject to inheritance. Further, it does not specifically define how the property of the remaining spouse will be ascertained or protected. Instead, the Act appears to turn a blind eye to the fact that in marriages, there might be joint or several acquisition of property. For instance, this manifests itself in the case of household belongings whereby, without any interrogation as to ownership, the law seems automatically to regard the whole of this property as forming part of the estate of a deceased man. It therefore proceeds to provide that in respect of this property, the customary heirs shall not be entitled to any share.[44] Rather, the wife shall be entitled to retain the household belongings used by her during the lifetime of the deceased.[45] Though the widow emerges to benefit, but it is as good as saying to her: "You can solely inherit this part of your husband's estate. You do not have to share it with the other beneficiaries." However, this assumption is erroneous as the wife may have her own share of that household property. In some cases, she might even be the sole owner of the household assets.

This position is compounded by the fact that apart from the Married Women Act of 1882, there is no clear law that provides for property regimes for all forms of marriage in Malawi. In most jurisdictions, spouses are given the choice to marry either in or out of community of property. Couples then choose whether to opt for a scenario where property is jointly owned or where each spouse owns what they bring into the marriage. Both scenarios mean that after the death of a spouse, what constitutes the estate will be determined by the property regime under which the couple married. In Malawi, courts have taken the position that to prove ownership of matrimonial property, a party has to show title which is usually evidenced by monetary contributions, in the form of receipts or substantial payment must be proved.[46] This disadvantages most women because usually their contribution to matrimonial property is largely through reproductive labour which is the care economy, such as child rearing, cooking and looking after the home.

iv. Insecurity Over Matrimonial Residence

The fourth problem relates to the shelter of the widow. On a commendable note, the Act intended to provide for roof for the wife even after the death of her husband.[47] In this regard, the customary heirs are given no entitlement to the doors, windows or other fittings of any house. However, the fact that the other beneficiaries under the Act (who include the children and the dependants under the Act) have not been excluded is cause for concern. The law seems to suggest that those beneficiaries can have a lawful claim to the fittings. In this regard, the law provides a leeway for property dispossession. On the one hand, dependants can be justified in claiming a share in house fittings and the beneficiaries to the estate, including heirs at customary law can be justified in chasing the widow away from the house by simply allowing her to take the fittings, while she leaves behind the structure. Under the same section[48], a widow holds her share of her deceased husband's estate on condition that if she re-marries, any subsisting property shall become divisible between her children by the deceased person upon fair distribution in accordance with Section 17. The degradation of the widow is so vivid in these circumstances. She is basically prevented from re-marrying as so doing would render her poor again based on the assumption that she was well off under the previous marriage. This is a fundamental violation of her autonomy as an individual to make decisions about her life, that is, whether to marry or not. In this regard, the Act is in violation of the widow's rights to an adequate standard of living, shelter and the right to marry.

4.4.2.4 Distribution of Property Belonging to a Deceased Woman

The Act[49] makes specific provisions for the distribution of the property of a deceased woman. The sole beneficiaries to her estate are her children. But where she dies without leaving children, the persons entitled to her property must be ascertained in accordance with customary law.

In dealing with the property of a woman who has died intestate, a problem arises where such woman is childless. The law states that in such a situation, the property should be distributed according to customary law. It might however be difficult to identify customary law which clearly defines how a woman's property is to be distributed and who should be her beneficiaries. In addition, it is difficult to ascertain satisfactory property rights of a woman at custom as her interests are not respected in favour of males. Reliance on customary law is therefore deceitful because it is the very custom that gives a leeway for men to exercise control over the woman and her property.

4.4.2.5 Distribution of Property Under Section 18

The Wills and Inheritance Act has a more equitable provision[50] which applies to two groups of widows. The section applies to an estate of a person domiciled in Malawi to whose estate customary law would not have applied even if the Act had not come into operation. Spouses of such deceased persons may benefit from the section. The section further applies to estates of immovable property belonging to deceased persons not domiciled in Malawi.

It is a gender neutral section that applies to estates of deceased men and women. The provision states that the surviving spouse of the deceased person shall be entitled to the first K10,000.00 of the estate. The remainder of the estate must be held in trust for the issue of the deceased person. But in the absence of such issue, if the deceased person is not survived by relatives, the remainder must go to the surviving spouse. But if he or she is survived by relatives, then the remainder must be split equally between the surviving spouse and the said relatives.

One problem with this section is that it may only be to the advantage of spouses whose deceased partners have left behind a small estate.[51] But for such survivors who are benefiting from a medium or large estate then the share of K10,000.00 would be very insignificant and clearly unfair. The figure has clearly been overtaken by economic trends and is very small.

In so far as the deceased spouse does not leave any issue, this provision can be said to adequately provide for the surviving spouse. In such a case, the spouse can be assured of inheriting the whole or half of the estate. However, taking into account the fact that the meaning of the word "issue" under the act is so broad, it is unlikely[52] that a surviving spouse would be in such a situation. This means that unless the law is re-visited, his or her common fate would be to inherit the equivalent of K10,000.00 from the estate of a deceased spouse.

4.4.2.6 The Two Distinct Provisions on Property Distribution

The widow, other beneficiaries or surviving spouse can only benefit either under section 16 or section 18. They cannot benefit under both sections. The tests for determining the governing provision for a particular beneficiary is whether customary law could, but for the Wills and Inheritance Act, have applied to the intestate property of the estate of the deceased person or not, or whether the deceased man in question was not domiciled in Malawi. If it would have, then the provision to follow is Section 16 as read with Section 17.[53] But if it would not have applied, then the estate is governed by section 18.[54] The question becomes, what factors determine whether customary law would have applied to a given estate or not? The act is not clear on this provision and therefore as such we have come up with two positions which may be applicable in this case.

4.4.2.7 Section 84 of the Wills and Inheritance Act

Section 84 is a recent amendment to the Wills and Inheritance Act. It was passed to criminalise the dispossession of property obtained by inheritance. Section 84 A provides that

"any person not being entitled thereto under a will or upon an intestacy who, in contravention of the Will or the Act takes possession or grabs, seizes, diverts or in any manner deals in or disposes of any property forming part of the estate of a deceased person or does anything in relation to such property which occasions or is likely to cause deprivation of any form or hardship to a person who is entitled thereto, shall be guilty of an offence and liable to a fine of K20,000.00 or to imprisonment for 5 years. In addition to such sentence, the court shall make an order directing that:

- *the property or monetary value thereof be immediately restored to the person or persons lawfully entitled thereto or to the estate of the deceased person;*
- *the whole or such part of the fine imposed as the court shall specify in the Order to be paid to the person or persons entitled or into the estate of the deceased person".*

In a nutshell, this section provides that the penalty for taking possession, grabbing, seizing, diverting or dispossessing a person of property forming part of the estate of a deceased person shall be K20,000.00 or imprisonment for 5 years. In the light of this provision, it can arguably be said that so long as it is proved that a person has:

- dispossessed a widow of property which has been disposed to her under a will;
- dispossessed a widow of household property which automatically vests in the widow on intestacy;
- dispossessed a widow of property which is awaiting distribution, in the case of intestacy notwithstanding that there are also others who are entitled to the same property;
- dispossessed a widow of property which has been distributed to someone else in the case of intestacy;

then there will be a case of property disposition.

However, the interpretation of the words 'not entitled thereto' as employed in this section might pose some challenges to the foregoing arguments. It might be argued that in the case of intestacy, dependants and heirs at customary law can not be prosecuted for the offence since they are "entitled" to the property forming part of an estate in one way or another. This is a shortfall in the section. The point of emphasis however is that such entitlement cannot arise until distribution. As long as such distribution is not effected, such individual cannot rightly claim to be entitled to the particular property which she or he has dispossessed, since that is a matter for the administrator to decide. This is so especially bearing in mind the fact that the wider estate belongs to so many beneficiaries.

In any event, no one, apart from the widow can claim entitlement to household belongings arising out of intestacy. However, experience has shown that most dispossessors fail to understand the concept of distribution and assume entitlement before such distribution has taken place. This is the thrust of the crime of dispossessing widows, therefore the section fails to address this point effectively. Section 84A ought to be invoked once anyone, though otherwise entitled, takes property before it is lawfully distributed to him or her.

The other set back in the provision in so far as enforcement is concerned is that the law only gives the mandate to the office of the Director of Public Prosecution (DPP) to prosecute the offence created under Section 84A. As such, prosecution of perpetrators of property dispossession under the Act is outside the jurisdiction of the police unless such permission is obtained by the DPP's office. However, for administrative purposes, this has proved to be quite difficult and has thus hampered the prosecution of offenders under this section. The office of the DPP is relatively small and understaffed and therefore choked with business.

4.5   Jurisdiction of Courts over Estates of Deceased Persons and Issues of Dispossession of Widows

Having examined the law regarding the dispossession of widows, this section seeks to examine how the central justice delivery system is constructed to deal with such law.

4.5.1   Jurisdiction of the High Court
The Constitution confers upon the High Court of Malawi unlimited original jurisdiction to hear and determine any civil or criminal proceedings under any law.[55] There are, however, more specific powers that the High Court can exercise with regard to issues of dispossession of widows.

4.5.1.1 Granting and Revoking Probate and Letters of Administration of Estates of Deceased Persons

Under the Wills and Inheritance Act,[56] the High Court has jurisdiction over all matters relating to probate and the administration of the estates of deceased persons. This includes power to grant probates of wills and letters of administration to such estates and to alter and revoke such grants. The power to alter and revoke grants can be of particular relevance to widows as victims of property dispossession. It can be invoked where a property dispossessor has obtained the grant for his/her own benefit. The victim can make an application to the court requesting the perpetrator to give an account of his/her administration. Should he/she fail to give satisfactory account, the court can accordingly revoke his/her grant.[57] The process is very costly and lengthy.

4.5.1.2 Power to Grant Interim Letters of Administration

The Wills and Inheritance Act further gives the court the power to grant interim letters of administration pending the granting of probate or letters of administration.[58] The effect of such a grant is to confer on the interim administrator all the rights and powers of a general administrator other than the right of distributing an estate of a deceased person. This may be necessary where no administrator has been identified or where there is urgent need such as where funds are needed for school fees or food. Such an application can be made without the knowledge of and in the absence of other concerned people.

The provision could be used by victims and potential victims of property dispossesion who may apply to the court for interim letters of administration if the estate is in danger of falling into the hands of property dispossessors. The fact that such application can be made in the absence of others helps to avoid clashes with potential dispossessors. On the other hand, the provision can also be easily abused and used to clothe property dispossession with some legality. This would be in a case where the property dispossessor who is likely to be a relation of the deceased person rushes to court to obtain the order in the absence of all other potential beneficiaries. Once the order is granted to him or her, he or she can deal with the property anyhow. This may result in the dispossession of the widow.

4.5.1.3 Appointment of Receivers Pending a Grant of Probate or Letters of Administration

The Wills and Inheritance Act also gives the High Court the power to appoint a receiver with the aim of protecting estates of deceased persons pending grant.[59] Such receiver may be appointed on the application of any person claiming to be interested in the property or having custody and control. The condition is such that there must be danger that such property may be wasted. If property forming part of an estate is dispossessed before distribution, chances are that such property will soon be wasted with the aim of defeating the rightful claims of other beneficiaries. Further, the fact that it can not be certain as to how the dispossessor intends to deal with the property, places such property in danger of being wasted. A victim of property dispossession should therefore be encouraged to make an application to court. As a receiver who has the mandate to avoid the wastage of property, the victim can claim back such property on behalf of the estate from the dispossessor, pending a grant of probate or letters of administration. This can work to the advantage of the widow in that where a will was left, she will be able to get her rightful entitlement and where there was no will, matrimonial property may be preserved for appropriate distribution.

Granting of Injunctions

In general, an injunction is an important remedy which works to the advantage of victims of property dispossession. It can even be obtained at the same time as the interim grant of letters of administration or receivership when there is urgent need to restrain the perpetrator from further dealing with the property.

The High Court has power to grant an injunction against property dispossessors restraining them from unlawfully inter-meddling with the estate of deceased persons. A victim can apply for an injunction without the knowledge and in the absence of the other interested parties. Such orders are normally made for a limited time pending an application to court at which time other interested parties may be heard too. If it is later proved to the satisfaction of the court that the injunction should be continued, the court grants a final injunction until letters of administration are obtained or, if the issues are contentious, until such issues are resolved at a trial.

For example, in a local case of the *Administrator-General (as administrator of the estate of Peter Thauzeni Chulu) vs Rajan Mudaliar and Mussa Gwira*,[60] the second defendant, being a relative of the deceased person, dispossessed a widow a house and several assets belonging to the estate of the deceased person before the Administrator-General, to whom letters of administration had been granted, had distributed the property. Though not included as a party, the second defendant was acting in unison with the widow's stepdaughter. The High Court granted an injunction to the Administrator-General restraining the defendants from their wrongful act.

4.5.2 Jurisdiction of Magistrates Courts

The Wills and Inheritance Act also gives the Minister of Justice the mandate to confer any jurisdiction on magistrate courts relating to estates of deceased persons which the magistrate is satisfied does not exceed K5,000.00 in gross value. This may include jurisdiction to grant probate or letters of administration in relation to such estates.[61] This means that magistrate courts do not have original jurisdiction to determine matters involving deceased estates and make grants unless with the sanction of the Minister of Justice. However, once such jurisdiction is conferred, the fact that it is afterwards discovered that the gross value of the estate exceeds K10,000.00 does not invalidate the magistrate's act in relation to the estate.[62] This is an important provision because in comparison to the High Court the magistrates courts are more accessible to the local populous than the former. However, the provision would have been even more helpful if the requirement for ministerial sanction was dispensed with so that the courts would have an unqualified mandate to deal with matters relating to small estates. Most of the disputes relating to estates of deceased persons at grassroots level involve very small estates anyway. Otherwise, it needs to be clarified as to whether the automatic power of the now non functional traditional courts to hear matters related to deceased estates[63] can now apply to the magistrates courts which have since been mandated to bridge the gap created by the abolition of the traditional courts[64].

The magistrates courts however have no jurisdiction to issue an injunction.[65] Hence the majority of people with no access to the High Court are at a disadvantage. The inter-meddler of deceased property may not be easily restrained from so doing with as much speed and ease, as is the case with those with access to the High Court.

However, the magistrates courts have similar power to make interim orders related to property which include protective orders and orders for sale of property for preservation.[66] Under the protective order the magistrate court can order for the delivery, preservation or custody of any movable property which is the subject matter of a dispute. How widely this power is exercised needs to be determined and assessed. It is however a provision that could greatly benefit victims of property dispossession.

Another unsatisfactory position regarding the jurisdiction of the magistrates courts is that they are excluded from having any jurisdiction over land matters.[67] The problem is again compounded by the position of the traditional courts. Although much of the land in areas with limited access to the High Court (which has jurisdiction in these matters) is customary land, the findings of our research shows that land, particularly customary, is high on the list of property which is a subject of dispute in estates of deceased persons.

4.6   Conclusion

The law relating to the dispossession of widows is far from meeting with Malawi's obligations under international, regional and national law as discussed in this chapter. It is high time that serious measures were taken to relook at this law for the benefit of widows who are the main victims under the current state of affairs. The law as it stands is a reflection of the legal status of women in Malawi. Despite constitutional guarantees it appears that legally women are yet to obtain equality with their male counterparts.

Lastly, courts' procedures are complicated for the average Malawian woman to follow and are also expensive. There is need for an accessible simple legal process to be put in place for the Malawian woman in order for her to realize her rights in respect of wills and inheritance matters.

[1] Adopted by the United Nations in 1948

[2] Section 11

[3] Section 211 of the Constitution of the Republic of Malawi

[4] Section 211 Supra, note 3

[5] Section 13 Supra, note 3

[6] Section 211 Supra, note3

[7] Kanyongolo, Edge: 2000

[8] Kanyongolo Supra

[9] Article 27

[10] Kanyongolo, Supra, note 3

[11] Ibid

[12] Section 11 (2) (c) provides that where applicable, the court of law shall have regard to current norms of public international law and comparable foreign law; Section 44 (2) provides no restrictions or limitations may be placed on the exercise of any rights or freedoms provided for in the constitution other than those prescribed by law, which are reasonable, recognized by international human rights standards and necessary in an open and democratic society.

[13] Adopted and proclaimed by the UN General Assembly in 1948

[14] article 1

[15] article 7

[16] article 17

[17] article 25

[18] adopted by the UN General Assembly in 1966

[19] adopted by the UN General Assembly in 1966

[20] The Republic Vs Chakufwa Chihana

[21] adopted by the UN General Assembly in 1979

[22] article 2 (c)

23 article 2 (f)

24 article 16 (H)

25 paragraph 32

26 article 18 (2)

27 The article states that the state shall ensure the elimination of every discrimination against women and also ensure the protection of the rights of the woman and the child as stipulated in international declarations or conventions.

28 Section 11 (2) (c)

29 Section 10

30 Section 16 (2) of the Wills and Inheritance Act, Laws of Malawi

31 Schedule to the Act which specifies the districts of Chitipa, Karonga, Rumphi, Nkhata Bay, Mzimba and Nsanje

32 Section 16 (2) (a) and (ii)

33 Section 16 (2) (b) (i)

34 Section 2 (i)

35 Section 17

36 Section 17 (i) a

37 *Ibid* as read with Section 17 (2) (b)

38 Section 17 (1) (c)

39 Section 2 (1)

40 Section 17 (i) (b) as read with section 16 (3)

41 Section 2 (1)

42 Section 17 (2) as read with Section 17 (1) (a)

43 Section 15

44 Section 16 (3)

45 Section 17 (i) (b)

46 Forrester vs Forrester, matrimonial cause No. 16 of 1993

47 Section 16 (3)

48 Section 16 (5)

49 Section 16 (4) (a)

50 Section 18

51 Under Section 2 (1) a small estate is defined as the estate of a deceased person consisting of property which does not exceed K20,000.00

52 Section 2 (1) provides that "issue" in relation to any person means the children, grandchildren and more remote descendants of that person.

53 Section 16 (l)

[54] Section 18 (1)

[55] Section 108 (1)

[56] Section 21

[57] Section 54

[58] Section 45

[59] Section 25

[60] (Malawi civil cause no. 1852 of 1999).

[61] Section 21 (3)

[62] Section 21 (4)

[63] Section 22 of the Wills & Inheritance

[64] WLSA Malawi 2000

[65] Section 39 of the Courts Act

[66] Under Order xxv of the subordinate Court Rules

[67] Section 39 (2) (b) of the Courts Act

Chapter Five
THE WIDOW DISPOSSESSED

5.1 Introduction

This chapter presents the research findings and observations on the process of dispossessing the widow. Dispossession of widows happens within a given socio-cultural context. We contend that dispossession relates to various processes that affect the status of women to culminate into property dispossession after the death of their spouses. The processes begin from the dynamics of patrilineal and matrilineal societies, which reinforce male superiority. The concept of family also recognises males as having the ultimate authority. Even in the arrangement of marriages, male status and ownership disempower women. Ultimately, when the husband dies, the construction of widowhood is a stepping-stone for relatives of the deceased man to dispossess the woman. This chapter therefore unveils the link between such social and cultural processes to property dispossession. It then discusses the dynamics involved in the actual dispossession itself after the death of a husband.

5.2   Social and Cultural Contexts of Matrilineal and Patrilineal Societies

Malawi has two lineage patterns, patrilineal and matrilineal. Under patrilineality, descent is through males, and residence is patrilocal.[1] The wife leaves her village and resides in her husband's village. On the other hand, in matrilineality, descent follows the female lineage. Marriages are matrilocal. The husband leaves his village and settles in the village of his wife and her mother.[2] In some cases, the wife resides at her husband's village. This is known as *chitengwa*, literally meaning *being taken*. This practice is very common in the Central Region of Malawi. In the matrilineal South, it is usually chiefs and heads of lineage (*mwini mbumba*) who practice *chitengwa* since they are expected to reside in their own villages. The dynamics of both patrilineality and matrilineality, as the study confirmed, manifest patriarchy.

49

5.2.1 *Dynamics of Matrilineality*

To understand the dynamics of matrilineality, much can be borrowed from the Chewa experiences as described by Phiri.[3] "Historically, in matrilineal society, a woman was looked upon as root of lineage *(tsinde)* and dependent *(mbumba)*. This shows that a woman was given a high status and a certain amount of freedom, but also at the same time heavily dependent on her male folk, usually her uncle and brother which was not there in patrilineal society. This was regardless of whether she was single or married. To illustrate her subordinate status, she was not spared from the evils of ritual intercourse during initiation, early marriages, mental torture to barren and single women, polygamy, levirate marriages and abusive widowhood rites. Thus the Chewa matrilineal society was also patriarchal."[4]

Despite this, the Chewa still recognised a woman as important in their society. She was recognised as the root *(tsinde)* of the lineage. Her value was therefore associated with having children. The personhood of a woman was not in her own right but in relation to what she could offer the community in terms of children. Particularly important were girl children as they continued with the lineage all over again. Due to this important role, the Chewa woman maintained close ties with her family. She also had the privilege to control, with the help of uncles and brothers, the offspring of her marriage and to retain rights of possession over them.[5] The significance of procreation made barrenness the greatest misfortune to befall a woman. Phiri quotes what John Mbiti has said about the barren woman – which is true for a woman in matrilineal societies.

> "Unhappy is the woman who fails to get children, for whatever other qualities she might possess, her failure to bear children is worse than committing genocide. She has become the dead end of human life, not only for the genealogically line but also for herself. When she dies, there will be nobody of her own immediate blood to remember her, to keep her in the state of personal immortality. She will simply be forgotten ... She will suffer for this, her own relatives will suffer for this, and it will be irreparable humiliation for which there is no source of comfort in traditional life."[6]

Today, similar dynamics prevail in the matrilineal societies including those of the Lomwe in Mulanje, the Yao in Mangochi and the Mang'anja in Chikwawa, where the research was conducted. The only marked difference is that women no longer enjoy the high status and freedoms they originally did. This makes the position of women in patrilineal and matrilineal societies equal in terms of powerlessness. When a husband dies, it is this state of powerlessness that makes it easy for relatives of her husband to dispossess her of property.

5.3 Paradigms of Dispossession

An analysis of the research findings reveals that dispossession of the widow is intrinsically linked to the following paradigms: socio-cultural construction of family, marriage, male status and widowhood. Each of these processes distinctively contributes to property dispossession of the widow in the wake of her husband's death.

5.3.1 Dispossession by the Socio-construction of "Family"
In both matrilineal and patrilineal societies, "family" is understood at two levels, namely nuclear and extended. At both levels, patriarchal values prevail. This results in the dispossession of a widow because the 'subordinate' status of women makes her defenseless against her in-laws.

The nuclear family comprises a father and a mother and any offspring. The extended family is dynamic, as it comprises blood relatives and those enjoined by marriage. The English term of family translates into two vernacular terms, namely *banja* and *mbumba*. While *banja* refers to the nuclear family, *mbumba* refers to the extended family. The person responsible for the extended family is referred to as *'mwini mbumba'* (owner of the lineage). He is the woman's uncle, grand-uncle or brother. In the absence of either, a brother takes the role. In this regard, the *'amalume'* is the custodian of all that belongs to the family. The husband rules his own household, *the nuclear family.*

At both the nuclear and extended family levels, the family only recognizes a man as the head of household. Women are considered subordinates, to be from their natal to their marital homes. This dispossesses them of power and control over property in the home. When the one in control, the husband, dies, their subordinate status paves way to property dispossession by their in-laws. The recognition of the extended family in itself also contributes to the widow's dispossession, since as part of a 'family', relatives at large are bound to have an interest in their deceased relative's property. Unfortunately, such interests are often realised without first considering the widow's interests in the property and sometimes realising that the widow has an interest in the property and disregarding it.

5.3.2 Dispossession Guaranteed by Marriage and its Arrangements
The process of marriage makes dispossession of the widow a certainty. Its arrangement involves certain formalities in both the matrilineal and patrilineal societies. In matrilineal societies, it involves the exchange of chickens by marriage advocates (*ankhoswe*). In patrilineal districts, marriage is validated by the payment of *lobola* (bride wealth). The way marriage is arranged in both societies endorses the low status accorded to the woman. The arrange-

51

ments emphasise on male superiority in the marriage and it is usually men who assume key roles. More particularly in the patrilineal societies, the payment of *lobola* relegates the woman's status in the marriage. This is because by virtue of marriage, she transfers all her reproductive and property rights to her husband and his kinsmen. The process of dispossession therefore gets rooted because of such disempowering arrangements. What actually happens when her husband dies is a climax of her disempowerment.

5.3.2.1   *Marriage Arrangements in Matrilineal Societies*

In the matrilineal societies visited, the prospective bridegroom's uncle or brother make marriage arrangements. They act as marriage advocates (*ankhoswe*), and propose officially to the prospective bride's family. This happens after the prospective bridegroom has already proposed to the prospective bride. On the prospective bride's side her uncle or brother represent her and her family. When proposing marriage, demeaning idioms are often used. The prospective bridegroom's advocate addresses his counterpart by saying *"tambala wathu anaona kamsoti pano, kaya takapeza?"* This translates, as "our cockerel is interested in a small hen that lives here, is it available?" Reference to a man as a stronger and bullying chicken, and a woman as a weaker and submissive chicken seals the woman's dispossession as a subordinate being from the inception of marriage. Marriage is considered constituted when all formalities are completed. In these societies, an exchange of chickens endorses the validity of the marriage.

It was disclosed that under the matrilineal system, the man is expected to reside in the woman's village. He is given a plot of land on which to build a house and another for farming so that he can fend for his family. A man may reside in his own village with his wife under the *chitengwa* arrangement. But even then, their wives and children are under the control of their own *mwini mbumba* (their mother's grand-uncle, uncle or brother). When taking the wife, the man is required to pay a token, usually a white chicken, to the guardian of his wife.

Traditionally, in matrilineal societies, men married at an older age. This was to allow themselves develop physical maturity to build a hut for the prospective wife. It also allowed the men to first work in their in-law's gardens and make enough domestic equipment to be used by themselves as well as the wives. They did this during courtship. The qualities and skills that a man would look for in a wife included: obedience, skilful cooking, and a good moral reputation.[7] This applies even today. While such requirements underline the husband's male superiority,[8] they also emphasise the woman's subordinate status. For instance, a wife's obedience is not only expected from her by a woman's husband, but also by all her in-laws. This type of obedience is one factor that leads to dispossessing the woman since it entails that she has to be an unequal partner at all times. Even in time of death, the widow is expected to display obedience to her in-laws to be seen as a woman with 'good qualities.' This includes obeying that they dispossess her of property. The *Chitengwa* arrangement increases the woman's vulnerability since she has the pressure of her in-laws to obey their word in their village. Her own family, which lives elsewhere, does not offer her immediate protection from dispossession.

5.3.2.2   Marriage Arrangements in Patrilineal Societies
The marriage arrangements in the patrilineal societies are signified by the payment of *lobola*. However, depending on whether the arrangements are made in the patrilineal societies of the north or south of Malawi, there are distinct processes that have to be followed. The entrenched *lobola* system, which is patriarchal in nature, leads to the degradation of women. There is a common belief that the wife has been bought. This same attitude influences in-laws to dispossess a widow of property. In their view, "a property", i.e. the woman, cannot own property. Some cultures believe that if anything the widow, as property, should also be inherited.[9] The system therefore forms the basis for women's discrimination, oppression and under-development, leaving women submissive and out of the decision making processes. All these factors lead to dispossession of the widow after her husband's death because the woman is not regarded as an independent being, capable of holding property rights other than being under the control of the husband and/or his family.

5.3.2.2.1   Northern Region Patrilineal Societies
The process of forming a *banja* in the patrilineal societies of northern Malawi visited happens when a man proposes marriage to a woman. Once the woman accepts the proposal, the man requests his relatives, particularly his uncles and brother, to visit the woman's family for the purpose of formally asking for her hand in marriage. He makes the request after consulting his aunt (*wankhazi*) on the woman's availability. The intermediaries in the marriage process are termed "*Thenga*", literally meaning messenger. When the woman's side is notified of the *Thenga's* intended visit, discussions commence with regards to making arrangements for the payment of *lobola*. According to the research participants, *lobola* is a symbol of the unification of the two families. It is viewed as a token of appreciation by the man's side to the woman's parents for bringing up the woman to marriageable age. *Lobola* also symbolises the physical transfer of the woman from her people to her husband's people, and the transfer of her reproductive rights and labour. Historically, *lobola* was paid in form of cattle. But due to modernisation, it is now also paid in monetary terms. A group discussion with 16 village headmen in Enukweni Village, Mzimba, revealed that the process usually entails the demand by the woman's family for a herd or

herds of cattle. The value of the cattle, usually converted into a monetary value, is then paid as the *lobola*. Depending on the means of the prospective husband and the amount demanded, the *lobola* can be paid in full or in installments. The full payment of *lobola* symbolises the formation of a valid marriage. The effect of exchanging *lobola* therefore is to allow the wife to leave her home to reside with her husband's people. In practice, if the parties marrying are faith believers, the payment of *lobola* is usually followed by a religious solemnisation of the marriage.

The *lobola* custom dispossesses the widow because by the time her husband dies, she is among her husband's kinsmen. These are the very people who believe that they bought her and that, as a result, she cannot have property in her own right. Consequently, her late husband's family controls all the property. In most cases if she chooses to leave, her entitlement to the matrimonial property is neither discussed nor considered. Basically she is expected to leave behind whatever property the couple had accumulated.

The Sena Patrilineal Society

In the Sena patrilineal research site of south Chikwawa, *lobola* has the same meaning as that in the northern districts of Malawi. However, the payment of *lobola*, though it symbolises marriage, has to be followed by another financial payment, *mpani*. This symbolises a permanent seal of the marital union. Another distinction is that under Sena marriage custom, the first step in arranging for a marriage is betrothal. When betrothing, the prospective husband pays to his prospective wife's family a fixed sum, which is termed "*Luphatho*"[10]. The man's a*nkhoswe* (marriage advocates) then go to the woman's family to inquire if their nephew has been accepted in marriage. If accepted, the *ankhonswe* will request the woman's family to take the betrothed woman to her prospective husband's home to visit for a few days. Such request is only a formality because in practice it is not denied, and her husband takes the betrothed woman. On the woman's return, her family will demand a specified amount of money as *lobola*[11] that should be paid by the prospective husband to claim the woman as his wife. The wife cannot go to live with her husband without this payment. But even then, the marriage is only truly sealed when the additional payment of '*mpani*' is paid. The *mpani* is in form of a goat and signifies true commitment of the husband to the wife for life. This requirement can be abused because there is no mandatory time frame within which the payment should be made. Therefore, so long as it remains unpaid, the husband has the right to refuse to make the payment and return the wife at anytime if she displeases him in any way. The abuse can also continue after the death of the husband. His relations can refuse to recognise the wife's status and use the fact that no '*mpani*' was paid as a ground to dispossess her of property.

54

There is a marked distinction in the ways marriage arrangements in matrilineal and patrilineal societies dispossess the widow. Despite this, it is clear that for both societies, formal arrangements are crucial to the 'existence' of a marriage. As established in Zambia, the fulfillment of all customary requirements relating to marriage usually determines whether or not a wife is eligible to inherit property. The dispossession of the widow can therefore commence once any flaw exists. However, 'valid' marriages need not only be arranged at custom. Marriages contracted under civil law, by permanent cohabitation and by repute are also as valid.[12] Emphasis on fulfillment of customary procedures to establish a marriage is therefore unconstitutional.

5.3.3 Male Status as a Dispossessing Tool

In this context, male status refers to the power accorded to men as husbands in both the matrilineal and patrilineal societies. In matrilineal societies, the matrilocal nature of marriages does not affect men's' control of their nuclear families and economic resources. In the patrilineal societies, men do not only have total control over their wives and property, but also automatic custody to children.

5.3.3.1 The Nkamwini and Mwini Mbumba Status in Matrilineal Societies

In the matrilineal societies, men disclosed that when they marry they are referred to as '*Nkamwini.*' This literally translates as 'that which belongs to another'. Some men, especially in Mulanje, disapproved of the word because it has connotations of being a stranger, someone who does not belong, and/or someone who is some kind of slave. The *mbumba* or extended family all belong to and are answerable to the maternal uncle (*mwini mbumba*), the custodian of his sisters' children. Under this arrangement, the '*mwini mbumba*' is culturally expected to look after the welfare of his sisters children and not his own. In turn, his children are the responsibility of their maternal uncle. He decides where the sister's husband shall build his house, where he will do his farming activities and also controls the children born in the family of his niece/sister or grand niece. However, the *nkamwini,* as husband, is the head of his own household. This arrangement contributes to a woman's dispossession because after the death of her husband, her in-laws have no obligation whatsoever towards the children. They therefore have no conscience against dispossessing the widow of property because they feel she and her children cannot benefit from the "property" of somebody who had no traditional duty to maintain them. The widow is expected to rely on her *mwini mbumba,* who has the ultimate responsibility to fend for the children.

Additionally, a general group discussion held in the area of Traditional Authority Jalasi in Mangochi expressed concern that the *chikamwini* custom prompts a husband (*nkamwini*) to be very conscious of the socio-economic developments he engages in his wife's village. For him to develop his household happily, he may prefer to move to a neutral place with his wife. This contributes to property dispossession, as it is easier for relatives to cause trouble at a neutral place[13] than the wife's own home. This is confirmed by the experiences of one young widow, Sara Gulani of ChoweVillage, T.A. Jalasi in Mangochi District.

Sara's husband passed away in June 1999. When they were just married, her late husband, who hailed from a nearby village, convinced Sara to move to a neutral area. They subsequently moved to Kachere, a peri-urban area in Blantyre District. In Kachere, the couple invested in a block of four houses for leasing to tenants, and a grocery shop, which Sara managed. After her husband's burial and the performance of all Islamic funeral rites, Sara's brothers-in-law ordered her not to return to her matrimonial home. Instead, they took over the home and all the investments at Kachere. They did not even give her a share in the property. Sara complained to the chief, who distributed the property. Sara and her children were given two houses. Her in-laws were given the other two houses and the grocery shop. After this, Sara was still advised by her in-laws to return to her home village. They undertook to be sending her rentals from her houses. However, this turned out to be deception as, at the date of the interview[14], her in-laws had still not sent her a penny. On her part, Sara could not do much. The neutral place, Blantyre, being so far away from Mangochi, she could not find transport money to go and collect the rentals herself.

Sara's in-laws disregarded the fact that they were receiving Sara's share in trust and therefore ought to have acted in her interests by paying over the money.

5.3.3.2   The Man: the Lord in Patrilineal Societies

The status of the man in the patrilineal societies is different. Due to the patrilocal nature of the marriage and the payment of *lobola*, the man enjoys superior status without any qualification. The children of the family belong to him and his kinsmen. The matrimonial property exclusively belongs to the husband. When a husband dies, the widow may be invited to stay. However, the research participants emphasised that the continuance to occupy the deceased person's home largely depends on whether or not the widow had children with the deceased man. On her own, she is of no use to the clan. The participants queried, '*what would she be doing here if there are no children?*' If the widow leaves her husband's village for whatever reasons, she cannot take any property with her. The issue of her own entitlement to some of such property is not even considered. This status totally dispossess the widow because she can only have an *indirect* interest in her property if she has children and continues to stay amongst her husband's kinsmen. Since this position is inherent in the nature of the arrangement of the marriage, the widow cannot later assert her rights to property when her husband dies. She is taken to have accepted her destiny when she entered into the marriage. The researchers therefore observed that the bargain that most married women make with patriarchy is unfair. They lose their identity, which makes it impossible for them or their families to argue for their property rights. As this chapter will further show, some of those who have dared to assert for their rights have faced sanctions from their in-laws. Therefore, the issue of superior male status is closely linked to ownership of property.

Cultural Dispossession through Property Ownership

The ownership of property in matrilineal and patrilineal societies is largely dependent on the dynamics of the respective societies. Since men have power and control in both societies, they inevitably dominate property ownership. In matrilineal societies, the *mwini mbumba* controls the land. The *nkamwini* as head of his household has power and control over the productive labour and all economic resources. This manifests itself through the genderisation of property prevailing in these societies. Property is labeled masculine and feminine depending on usage and value. For instance, a bucket is considered a woman's property while a bicycle is a man's property. This happens both at divorce and during the distribution of property after death. In the patrilineal societies, since marriages are patrilocal, the male side controls the property.

5.3.4.1 *Rights in Property during Marriage*
In both the matrilineal and patrilineal systems, both the men and women stated that the male member of the household controlled matrimonial property amassed during the marriage. The property is generally labelled as belonging to the man. The man exerts authority over the distribution of financial and material resources. In matrilineal societies, this applies even where the resources have been realised from the sale of proceeds from the very land that belongs to the woman's clan. The female participants' views on ownership were divided. Some felt that property acquired during the marriage belongs to both spouses. Others felt that it belongs to the man. Those who felt that matrimonial property belongs to the man did not see the need to question the authority exerted by the male side in matters of matrimonial property administration. To them, the buying power of the man determines ownership. On their part, the women down-played their contribution to the family welfare through reproductive labour such as cooking, gathering fuelwood, drawing water and looking after children, whilst the man was in paid employment.

The participants in the matrilineal districts of Mulanje and Mangochi stated that culturally the property is supposed to be categorized as feminine or masculine. This may be referred to as *genderisation of property*. The masculine property includes the man's clothes, wireless, car, livestock, beds, canoes bicycles and chairs. The feminine property includes the woman's clothes and kitchen utensils.

The categorizing of property into masculine and feminine is problematic because the splitting of the property is biased against the woman. She does not benefit from the masculine things that usually have a high monetary value. This is because ownership is premised on value and actual purchase and not contribution through services like cooking and home care, which are usually rendered by women. The narratives from the women in the research areas revealed that they are caught in the vicious cycle of poverty, which is largely due to their subordinate status to men. Kanyongolo[15] rightly argues that the society is framed in such a way that it gives men more access to the means of generating more income than it does women. Men have better access to education, employment, credit and land than women. In the vast majority of domestic relationships, therefore, women are dependent on resources generated by men and the death of the latter is the death of the bread-winner. It is through partnership of marriage that the women have access to the property and support the procurement of the material goods through unpaid labour, since such labour is deemed "not real" and not valuable.[16] In as long as modern economics refuses to put value on women's labour, women will always be relegated to a status of poverty. This is the thrust of the problem because upon divorce or death of a spouse, women lose access to the matrimonial property and their stake in the ownership of the same is hardly recognised because they do not normally have the purchasing power.

In the patrilineal societies visited, division of property does not exist. The woman does not have any property rights. In the lifetime of the husband, he has the control. Her own contribution is even accredited to her husband. This was revealed in a group discussion with chiefs in Enukweni. They stated that when given anything by their daughters, the one they thank is their son-in-law because that is his property. This mentality prevails in other patrilineal jurisdictions in the region. This supports research findings in Mozambique on a study on inheritance. In the patrilineal societies of Mozambique the paying of *lobola* (bridewealth) signifies that all the property belongs to the man. The property is also regarded the product of his labour while for the woman her goods include the crops which she cultivates (although in practice this also belongs to the man because of the *lobola* payment). The only things that a woman owns are her jewelry and marriage gifts, which are usually kitchen utensils.[17] This symbolises dispossession because the same situation will apply when her husband dies. Unlike in Mozambique, where a woman gets kitchen utensils as of right, the woman in the patrilineal societies of Malawi will usually get these depending on the goodwill of her late husband's family.

The cultural determination of property ownership in both matrilineal and patrilineal societies does not augur well with the new Malawi constitutional order. It takes away the rights of the woman, which are part of human rights protected under the Constitution. These include the right to fair disposition of property that is held jointly with the husband upon divorce[18] and the right not to be deprived of property obtained by inheritance.[19] This means that the widow is legally entitled to her prescribed share at all times. More importantly, the woman has the right to own property whether independently or in association with others.[20] Oppressive customary laws that determine property rights according to sex are therefore dispossessing. Dispossession of widows is clearly a fundamental violation of human rights. All customary laws that perpetuate it are invalid[21] and should be challenged.

5.3.4.2   *Distribution of Property on Divorce or Death*
In the matrilineal sites visited, on divorce or property distribution after death, all the masculine items go to the husband or his family and all the feminine things go to the wife or her family. Since the land for farming belongs to the woman's family, it is not tampered with. The house built at the wife's home is also usually left to her and the children. If there is a dispute over the house, it can be demolished and the iron sheets, due to their monetary value, split between the two families.

In patrilineal societies, the man holds total ownership of property. After his death, the control vests in his father or brothers. The widow is required to stay in her husband's village and use the property there. She cannot collect any household items to start afresh in her own village. To her late husband's family, a widow cannot 'start' all over again by herself. If she opts to leave, then she is thought to have planned to re-marry. She cannot therefore get anything if she leaves. The assumption is that any property that was amassed during the marriage was exclusively acquired by and/or for the husband. Even when it is accepted that the property exclusively belonged to the deceased husband, the wife is not allowed to have her share in his estate. This customary practice infringes on inheritance laws that recognizes that the widow has a stake in her husband's estate.[22] Through the practice, relatives of the deceased man perpetrate economic violence against the widow.

From the research findings, the recognition that women can be entitled to property in their own right seems far-fetched. On the death of a spouse, the woman's contribution to the joint estate is subsumed within the assumptions of male ownership and control. This male-driven assumption dispossesses the widow. Yet women are mostly the ones that contribute to the wealth of the family through labour in the fields, farm management and other jobs.[23] If the women are considered, it is only in respect to particular resources. Due to male dominance, women are expected to control minor resources which are seen as necessary and fitting for them because these are the resources which they need most to conduct their daily chores around the home.[24] As such, in times of divorce or death, women are expected to inherit those minor resources of little or no monetary value, contrary to the constitutional right to acquire and maintain rights in property whether independently or not.[25] Distribution of property according to inheritance laws is also neglected.

Cultural Dispossession through the Social Construction of Widowhood

In both matrilineal and patrilineal societies visited, a wife has a stake, whether directly or indirectly, in the matrimonial property after the death of her husband. Such stakes, however, are dependent on widowhood. The Oxford Dictionary defines a widow as a woman whose husband has died and who has not re-married. This implies that legally, a widow is a woman whose husband has died during the subsistence of marriage, regardless of whether at the time of death the couple were living together, or were legally separated, or were in the process of divorce. At custom, widowhood is not viewed so simplistically. Among the patrilineal Tonga of Malawi,[26] widowhood is defined as a status bestowed on a widow by her late husband's family at the death of her husband. This definition cuts across most cultures. Eligibility for widowhood depends on several factors.

5.3.5.1   Good Conduct

The 'widow's' conduct, both during her husband's lifetime and after his death, determines whether or not her in-laws will bestow the widowhood status on her. In the case of Mrs. Kulekana initially dealt by WLSA Malawi National Office in 1999 and which story was part of the publication by WLSA,[27] the relatives of her deceased husband were of the view that Mrs. Kulekana was a 'whore' and a 'slut,' not deserving of the widowhood status since she had not behaved "properly" during the deceased man's illness. This was in specific reference to the fact that the widow had continued to run the family business, which sometimes took her away from home, during her husband's illness. They therefore felt she deserved to be dispossessed of the property. These sentiments were expressed at the district assembly's office in Zomba, where the widow had lodged a complaint. In Zambia, a study on inheritance found that 'being of good conduct' also applied to the relationship between the widow and her in-laws. As a marriage expectation, the widow also had to be good to the husband's relatives during and after the lifetime of the husband.[28] Non-fulfillment of this expectation meant that the widow could not qualify for the widowhood status, and therefore property inheritance.

5.3.5.2 Fulfillment of Marriage 'Formalities'

The fulfillment of marriage formalities is another factor that influences the qualification of widowhood. To the interviewees, 'formal' marriage arrangements meant strict compliance with customary marriage arrangement formalities. Where parties are living together without compliance with such 'formalities', the woman has usually ended up losing all her inheritance rights, resulting in property dispossession. The period within which the parties may have stayed in the union does not matter.

Recognised formal marriage arrangements include having marriage advocates in matrilineal societies and paying full *lobola* in the patrilineal societies of Malawi's Northern Region. In the patrilineal Sena areas, it means the payment of *mpani* after the initial *lobola* payment. If the couple just registered their marriage or was simply cohabiting, the legitimacy of the marriage is denied. This is used as a ground of discrediting the woman. Widowhood is therefore not bestowed on her and her inheritance rights are not recognized. These results are similar to those in Botswana. There, in one case, it was reported that the step-children dispossessed their step-mother of all the property by capitalising on the informal manner in which the marriage was celebrated.[29] In another Tswana case, relatives of a deceased man dispossessed a widow who had cohabited with her deceased partner for well over 20 years.[30] The reason given was that as the marriage was unknown at custom, the widow could not be entitled to any inheritable property. In Malawi, the Republican Constitution may lead to a departure from this stringent requirement for a formal customary union. The constitution recognises informal marriage arrangements such as marriage by permanent cohabitation or by repute.[31] This automatically overrules the customary requirement.

5.3.5.3 Rituals Accompanying Widowhood

There are certain rituals that have to be observed by the widow in her status. These are mourning and cleansing rituals. These two rituals emphasise the widow's subordinate status to her in-laws. They disempower and dispossess the widow with regards to issues of her own matrimonial property.

i. The Mourning Ritual

Upon the death of a husband, the mourning period causes devastating circumstances for the widow. This is the time when the deceased husband's relatives usually mobilise themselves to dispossess the widow of property belonging to the family. As part of observing this ritual, the widow's behaviour during the period of mourning is monitored strictly by her deceased husband's relatives in order to use it as a basis for dispossessing her. Generally, in Malawi it is believed that when death occurs, the widow as well as other female mourners are expected to display their grief openly by wailing inconsolably, talk softly, dressing as befitting the solemn occasion (head scarf and a wrap around locally known as *chitenje*) and not engage in any type of confrontational activities. Inability to display such behaviour conveys an important message that the widow is not sorrowful and is hard-hearted. Sometimes, it relays the message that she deliberately killed her husband. In most cases, this automatically determines how her in-laws will consider the widow's rights to property. Similarly, among the Bemba of Zambia,[32] the widow is expected to wail and show significant grief. If she does not cry out loudly she is accused of behaving like a 'white woman' and sometimes she is accused of having caused her husband's death and may affect her right to inherit certain things.[33] Therefore, in order to be seen as a good woman, a widow would not normally resist any dispossession during the mourning period because of the dispossessing societal expectations, and not necessarily because of a woman's own weakness.

The mourning ritual can sometimes be very abusive and degrading. In some patrilineal societies in Dedza, a widow has to crawl all the way to the grave-yard, no matter how far.[34] Similar dehumanising rituals were revealed in a study carried out in Botswana.[35] It is reported that after the burial of a husband, one widow was not allowed to enter the house and had to sleep on the veranda. The next day, she was stripped naked and was only left with her petticoat. She was brought into the open and was made to lie down. Other widows proceeded to rub ointment provided by a witch doctor all over her body in the presence of everyone. She was later taken into the house but was made to walk while facing backwards, and wearing only one shoe. As she walked, she was made to chant '*I am walking backwards because I am a child; I am wearing one shoe because I am a child.* And then she was made to hit the walls of the house with a pestle while shouting '*I am pounding the walls because I am a child...*' The rationale behind this ritual is that a child or a lesser human being could not be entrusted with property in the absence of a man. Besides, in her situation, the widow is under the total control of her in-laws and has to comply with 'custom.' She is only told what will be done, how and by whom. This is a manifestation of 'obedience', to which the widow committed herself at the time she was getting married. For this reason, some female members of the traditional patrilineal Nnobi of Nigeria rightly viewed the mourning ritual as a punishment.[36] Men do not practise this ritual. This raises the presumption that due to male status, unlike women, men are regarded as clean by nature. On the other hand, they possibly recognise the ritual as a form of punishment. Being the major perpetrators of the ill practice, men therefore cannot punish themselves.

In all of the countries where WLSA has offices, mourning rituals for the widow involve restrictions on her behaviour and mobility. As a result, the widow in confinement for mourning purposes may not be able to protect her interests over the deceased estate. The phenomenon of dispossession and unlawfully accessing and distributing an estate may be carried out while she is closeted away in the process of ritual mourning.[37] During such moments even the family system does not seem to offer the necessary protection because of the belief that 'this is a mourning period.' Protection of property during this time is an unacceptable form of behaviour. Even when the period is over, the widow is still not in a position to defend her rights. She has yet to go through a liberating ritual, known as "cleansing."

ii. The "Cleansing" Ritual

"Cleansing" literally means making clean what was dirtied and/or defiled. This implies that the death of her husband makes the widow dirty. This is disempowering in itself because a dirty person is looked upon with contempt in society. A widow then cannot be fully accepted as a woman in society until she is "cleansed."[38] The "cleansing" ritual is therefore directly linked to property dispossession because in her state, the widow is not expected to take part in important discussions, including that involving property. Further, the fact that the ritual is controlled by the widow's in-laws, gives them a powerful weapon to dispossess the widow whether by force, or without any consultation.

In Traditional Authority Nthilamanja's area in Mulanje, one destitute widow revealed that the "cleansing" ritual entails that a widow has to sleep with one of her late brother's male relations. For this widow, this ritual resulted in the procreation of a child, whose father remains unknown up to date. Research findings in Zambia[39] have shown that the relatives of the deceased man have actually been known to take advantage of these rituals to dispossess the widow of property. Like in most societies in Malawi, among the Zambian Lozi, the "cleansing" ritual is highly valued. The widow's in-laws conduct this ritual. A widow may therefore not want to annoy her in-laws by fighting for property since they can opt not to "cleanse" her as a way of punishment.[40] She may therefore easily forego her property rights than risk being sanctioned. This fear is founded, because in our findings, Mrs. Newa, a Malawian widow in the patrilineal societies who dared resist her in-laws, faced such sanctions.

Mrs. Newa had been married for ten years when her husband passed away. Then, she was working as a clerk at one of the government's departments. Her husband had been working in the Department of Forestry. The couple had four children, with the youngest one being less than one year old when the husband died. The husband's remains were laid to rest among his people at his village in Rumphi District. After her husband's funeral rites, Mrs. Newa was requested by her in laws to stop working and stay in the village to look after her mother-in-law. She was told that her in-laws suspected that if she returned as a widow she was likely to engage in promiscuous behaviour. However Mrs. Newa refused to comply with their request, as she want-

ed to go back to work. This forthright refusal angered her in-laws. They escorted her to her house, and dispossessed her of some property. The in-laws were also responsible for the performance of cleansing rituals to release her from her widowhood (Chokolo) status. This would have made her a single person, free to re-marry. However, up to the time of the interview, two years after her husband's death, this, ritual had not been performed and her in-laws were still regarding her as a chokolo. Accordingly, she was still married to her late husband's clan and she could not have a relationship with another man, as this would be tantamount to adultery.

The two rituals show that custom creates widowhood in the most disempowering way to the woman possible. As such, it is difficult for a widow to assert her rights over property immediately after the death of her husband. During this period, issues of property are put out of her concern. Instead, society dictates that the issues be governed by her in-laws, who find a leeway to dispossess her.

5.4   Dispossession in Practice

The study revealed that dispossession of widows occurs both in matrilineal and patrilineal societies. While dispossession was acknowledged to be rampant in matrilineal societies, the participants in the Northern Region indicated that the level of dispossession in their societies is low. This was attributed to the fact that widows settle in their husband's village after the death of their husband. They are allowed to retain the property unless they opt to leave. However, it will be shown[41] that even this is an indirect form of dispossession of widows. Dispossession is understood from different perspectives in the matrilineal and patrilineal societies.

5.4.1 Grounded Perceptions of Dispossession

The definition of 'dispossession' in the matrilineal research sites is wider than that in patrilineal societies. In all the matrilineal research sites, property dispossession was defined as taking of property by relatives of a deceased spouse from a wife/husband and/or children without their consent, after the death of a spouse. Dispossession relates only to such property that the nuclear family had and was using before the death of the spouse. Among the patrilineal research sites of the Northern Region, dispossession of widows was understood to mean the forceful acquisition of property by relatives of a deceased man from his surviving spouse. In vernacular, dispossession translates as *kulanda chuma cha masiye*. The perception in matrilineal societies includes use of deceit and other indirect means to take property. In the patrilineal societies, the perception is restricted to forceful physical dispossession.

However, in both patrilineal and matrilineal societies, the fact that dispossession is not only confined to the property of the deceased person but to the whole matrimonial property is overlooked. This is done by totally disregarding the widow's entitlement. In Machinjiri, in Blantyre District, participants justified this practice by saying *that all property has to be distributed after the death of a man without settling the widow's entitlement because it was the man that was the head of the household.* However, this is a weak excuse, as the man's status does not rob the wife of the right to own property in her own capacity.

5.4.2 Victims and Perpetrators of Dispossession
Dispossession affects the female sex more than it does the male. Similarly, most of the perpetrators are males. It is a form of gender-based violence.

5.4.2.1 *Victims*
In both matrilineal and patrilineal societies, widows were identified as common victims of property dispossession, compared to widowers. Even most of the key informants in the justice delivery structures admitted that they had never received complaints from widowers. For example, the district assembly office in Mangochi stated that they receive about twenty cases per month from widows only. An official from Chikwawa District Assembly's Office also admitted that victims of property dispossession are usually widows. The official observed that during his five years handling of such cases, the office had only received one case from a widower. By virtue of this fact, all the interviewees were of the view that this conduct was a form of gender-based violence. This is because the women's right to own and manage property is violated although violent acts may not always be used.

5.4.2.2 *Perpetrators*
Most of the perpetrators in cases of property dispossession are men. It is in very few cases that women are involved. The identity of the perpetrators varied from site to site. In matrilineal societies, perpetrators are said to range from *ambuye* (uncles), brothers, parents and even nephews. Although the sisters of the deceased husband do not, on the face of it, feature among the list of the perpetrators, the study among the Lomwe in Mulanje found that when nephews dispossess the widow, the sisters of the deceased husband are normally the driving forces. This stems from the custom prevailing in matrilineal societies that nephews and nieces are the responsibility of their uncle. When the uncle dies, the cultural practice in Mulanje is to refer to his property as *'za ambuye'*. Translated literally, this means 'that which belongs to our uncle'. The nephews therefore take it for granted that their uncle's responsibility, and whatever was accumulated by him during his lifetime was for their benefit. When he dies, their mothers indirectly encourage them to take 'their' property from the widow. Sometimes, even before the death of the uncle, their mother may incite them to spy on the conduct of the wife so that later they can find an excuse to dispossess the widow. Some women,

therefore, oppress other women. This could be attributed to women's struggle over scarce resources. At the end of the day, it is the sisters who use the property. But on the other hand, the sisters behave in this way because they know that sooner or later, it will happen to them. This finding underscores similar findings in the Zambia study.[42] A study on inheritance revealed that dispossession of widows is sometimes largely dependent on the social-cultural values on property rights of individuals within that community depending on whether the community in question is matrilineal or patrilineal. Such values somehow promote dispossession because they foster a genuine belief in the relatives of the deceased man that it is their right, not the widow's, to inherit what they deem is the estate of their deceased relative. Unfortunately, the nephews among the Lomwe do not consider the widow's entitlement before taking the property.

In the patrilineal societies, the role that sisters play in dispossessing the widow is clearer. It was revealed that it is usually the parents, brothers, sisters and the uncles of the deceased person who dispossess the widow and leave her destitute. In the Northern patrilineal societies, these are sisters who ordinarily live in their natal village, and are purportedly very powerful amongst their own kinsmen. Other sisters get involved when they come back to live among their clan after divorce or death of their husbands. Their arrival causes conflicts because they themselves come empty-handed. The clan sisters feel that the sister-in-law, the widow, has taken over what was rightfully theirs (their brother's property). They therefore make her life difficult in order to drive her away. And if the widow opts to leave, they, through their brothers and father, do not allow her to take anything.

The dominant perpetrators are nevertheless the males. These assume the role of administrators. In that role, they are required to look after the welfare of the widow and children. However, the majority fails to carry out their duties. Instead of protecting the estate, the customary administrators serve their own interests at the expense of the dependants of the deceased person. The customary appointment of administrators contravenes the legal requirement that an administrator should be appointed by the High Court.[43] The fact that the administrator acts without those powers puts them in the position of a receiver. However, even the receiver must be appointed by the High Court.[44] This makes the customary *administrator's* authority legally unacceptable. He can therefore be sued for intermeddling with the estate of the deceased person.

5.4.3   The Process of Dispossession from Death to Distribution

The death of a husband marks the climax in the dispossession process, which arises from the social-cultural dynamics. It paves way for the actual dispossession, which in itself takes place in several stages. Some of these stages are common in both matrilineal and patrilineal societies. Dispossession takes place either directly or indirectly.

5.4.3.1 *Direct Dispossession Stages*

Direct dispossession refers to circumstances where dispossession takes place with the full realisation whether on the part of the victim or perpetrator, or both, that the property is being wrongfully taken from the widow without considering her entitlement. There are four stages in this regard.

5.4.3.1.1 *During Illness*

Dispossession sometimes occurs while the husband is ill. In Mulanje, this happens where the illness in question is of such a nature that there is virtually no hope of recovery. While the woman is nursing her husband's illness at the hospital, her in-laws may start selling goods at the matrimonial home. By the time the wife finally gets home, which will usually be after the husband has died, there will be nothing valuable or little else left. Such instances normally occur where relatives are afraid of facing resistance from the wife or would actually be embarrassed to dispossess her personally. They possibly opt to act during illness because they sometimes recognise that the matrimonial property was acquired through the joint effort of their brother and wife. Another finding in Mangochi showed that the dispossession at this stage is motivated by male dominance. Sometimes, male relatives of the deceased take advantage of the helplessness of the ill head of household to intimidate their in-law into surrendering the property into their hands. An example is the case of Ethel Yusuf:

Ethel was married to Mr. Yusuf for four years until his death in November 1999. While married the couple had one child who unfortunately passed away during infancy. The couple were living with a grown up relative of the husband. When the husband was ill and confined in hospital, Ethel was invited by his employers to collect his salary, which amounted to about K13,000.00 so that it could assist them during the illness. When she got home, the nephew demanded that she hand over the salary to him for safe-keeping. Mrs. Yusuf handed over the money because she felt intimidated and wanted to avoid conflicts with her in-law. However, after obtaining the money the nephew disappeared from the matrimonial home and only remitted to her K100.00 every week to buy household necessities. Under the financial difficulties created by the nephew's behaviour, she was compelled to borrow a sum of K2,000.00 from her husband's employers to meet the cost of food and medication.

As in Zambia, submission to dispossession is not usually voluntary. It is done out of the fear of ruining relationships with in-laws. Primarily, this is because culturally, the families of the deceased person are still very important in the performance of certain rituals, like 'cleansing'.

5.4.3.1.2 *During Bereavement*

Bereavement is the second stage used to dispossess the widow in both the matrilineal and patrilineal societies. The relatives target the widow's most vulnerable period to effect dispossession.

Women in Jalasi, Mangochi, reported that during mourning, it was all too common for women to be stripped of all matrimonial property and be left with nothing. Mirriam Duwe[45], who had such experience stated that when she was being dispossessed of her property at this stage, she was so bereaved by her husband's death that it was impossible for her to raise up issues of sharing the property that she and her husband had jointly accumulated. She just watched helplessly in disbelief.

In Mzuzu, Mrs. Newa narrated that when she refused to stay at her husband's home to look after her mother-in-law, her in-laws escorted her back to the matrimonial house in Mzuzu City. There they took most of the household items from her, including brand new iron-sheets for use in constructing a home. Mrs. Newa's reaction to this move was to plead with them to leave the iron-sheets behind, as she needed them to complete the construction of a house. Fortunately, after some struggles the in-laws heeded her pleas and only took the household assets. However, the in-laws did not take the children of the marriage with them in accordance with the requirements of the *lobola* custom. Because they ignored their duty, Mrs. Newa was therefore left with four children and the matrimonial home, which was emptied of all household goods.

The taking away of the household goods was clearly a breach of the provisions of the Wills and Inheritance Act, which provides that all household belongings automatically vest in the widow upon the death of her husband. They are not distributable. The taking of this property was therefore a clear commission of the crime of property dispossession under section 84 A of the Wills and Inheritance Act.

5.4.3.1.3 *Relocation of the Widow*

In matrilineal societies, it was revealed that property dispossession sometimes takes place when the widow's in-laws compulsorily make the widow relocate from the matrimonial home. This usually happens if the widow and her husband were staying at a *neutral* place. This refers to circumstances where the marriage is not strictly observing the *Chikamwini* nor *Chitengwa* residential arrangements. At this point the widow is the most vulnerable as she lacks the immediate protection of her family, and even well meaning in-laws.

The research revealed that in displacing the widow, the relatives of the deceased person simply chase her and children from the matrimonial home. Once she is out of the way, they take over the household and other businesses that the family was running. The case of Sara Gulani, who was chased away from her neutral home in Kachere, manifests the realities of this stage of dispossession. Her grocery shop business and houses were all taken over by her in-laws. Another widow who was indirectly displaced is Miriam Duwe from Jalasi Village in Mangochi. The displacement of Miriam was indirect because she was not chased out of the matrimonial home. Rather, she was still at her husband's home village, mourning.

Miriam comes from Mangochi District. Her late husband came from Balaka District. Their marriage was arranged in accordance with custom. Instead of settling at Miriam's village, the couple settled at Mangochi Boma where they jointly ventured into a business, operating passenger transport services in and around Mangochi District. They also grew crops at her husband's village in Balaka. Their business was so successful that at the time of the husband's death, the two had three mini-buses, two pick-ups, one motorcycle, and 70 sheets of corrugated iron sheets. Miriam described how she and her husband planned to operate their business. She was usually responsible for managing the income from the various vehicles. She regarded herself as having a vested interest in that property. When her husband fell ill in 1999, she decided to nurse him at his village in Balaka. Unfortunately, he was not ill for long and he passed away in September 1999. The following month, her father-in-law escorted her from Balaka and dropped her at Mangochi Boma and told her to find her way to her village. This was contrary to custom, which demands that she should be formerly handed over to her people during nsudzulo. Miriam was not given anything, but was only told that she would be contacted at a later date to discuss issues of property distribution. She was not even allowed to go back to her husband's village and harvest the maize and cassava crops which she and her late husband had cultivated. At the time of the interview, she still had not been contacted.

Though Miriam was sent back home from her late husband's village, the fact that she was not allowed to go back to the matrimonial home at Mangochi *Boma* amounted to compulsory relocation. It is worth noting that had Miriam and her husband followed the *chikamwini* system a lot of these problems that Miriam was experiencing would have been prevented. It would have meant that, at least, Miriam would have had her own house at her village. The fields could have been at her village. In any case, the *nsudzulo* ceremony would have accordingly taken place and the property would have been distributed properly.

The attitude of in-laws who displace widows signifies that they fail to appreciate the difference between matrimonial property that was held jointly by the couple and the personal property that was accumulated by the deceased individually. In the case of jointly owned property, the widow's share has to be determined before the property is distributed. Even in respect of the husband's individual property, distribution has to take into account the widow's

69

interest as prescribed by the Wills and Inheritance Act. For Sara and Miriam and their children, it would have meant their inheritance of 2/5 of the respective deceased husband's estate, over and above their other legal entitlements.

5.4.3.1.4 Personating the Widow

The relatives of the deceased husband sometimes engage in deceit and impersonation to dispossess the widow. In terms of institutional funds, some of the offices of the district assemblies stated that sometimes the relatives of the deceased husband conspire to exclude the widow as a beneficiary of death benefits. In such a case, the relatives bring a different person to act as the rightful widow or child of the deceased when collecting the funds. Mrs. Ethel Yusuf was dispossessed at this stage. She narrated:

After Mr. Yusuf's death, his employer, in conjunction with the Blantyre District Assembly, prepared a list of dependants and beneficiaries of his death benefits that included Mrs. Yusuf, her husband's nephew, her husband's girlfriend, Ms. Fatima Jali, and her two children. When Mrs. Yusuf visited the office of the Administrator-General to collect her share of the death benefits, she was shocked to be informed that her name was not among the list of beneficiaries and that Fatima Jali had collected money as a wife of the deceased person. It was Mrs. Yusuf's conviction that the nephew of her deceased husband had conspired with the girlfriend to have Mrs Yusuf, erased from the list of beneficiaries. As a result, the Administrator-General treated the girlfriend as the lawful and only wife of the deceased person for purposes of distributing the property. The nephew and the girlfriend used the money they had obtained from the estate of Mr. Yusuf to set up a jointly run bottle store in Ndirande Township. This economic venture substantiated Mrs. Yusuf's allegation that there was a conspiracy between the nephew and Fatima Jali to deprive her of her husband's death benefits.

The same nephew dispossessed Mrs. Yusuf during the illness of her husband. The fact that this time he dispossessed her at institutional level shows that there is serious laxity in the procedures used by the Administrator-General to disburse benefits. Through such negligence, the office facilitated the dispossession of the widow.

5.4.3.2   Indirect Dispossession Stages

Indirect dispossession of widows takes place through customary practices and institutional prescription of death benefits to beneficiaries. Normally, these stages of dispossession are accepted by society. However, the research revealed that they are so full of injustice that their ultimate effect on the widow is dispossession. They comprise five stages.

5.4.3.2.1 *During* Nsudzulo

Nsudzulo is a custom that is followed by matrilineal societies. This is the name given to the customary ceremony whereby a widow or widower is traditionally relieved of their widowhood status and set free to re-marry. Property is distributed during this ceremony. In a predominantly Lomwe ethnic site in Mulanje, the procedure during *nsudzulo* was described by one male participant as follows:

"When a husband dies and all funeral rites have been conducted, before people disperse, the relatives of the deceased person advise everybody of a date when nsudzulo *will be conducted. Meanwhile, they prepare an inventory of all the property that is in the house. On the specified day, the ceremony of* nsudzulo *is conducted first. The village chief is invited to such ceremonies as an observer and he can only intervene when there are quarrels. The deceased person's uncle or sometimes his nephews chair this ceremony. Then the deceased's uncle inquires about the property by addressing the widow and his relatives as follows* 'munthu wathu anasiya kabudula wake pano, tingamuone?' *(This literally translates as: our departed son left behind his shorts and we want to have a look at the same). This is a metaphorical way of saying that now let us distribute the property that we listed earlier on. The relatives of the deceased man assume the role of distributors and more often than not, they take most of the property and leave the widow with worthless items. In so far as they act is this way, such conduct amounts to property dispossession."*

The way the ceremony is conducted among the Lomwe should be contrasted to the procedure followed among the Yao in the Mulanje and Mangochi districts. Chief Apochele of Nthiramanja Village, Mulanje, describes the procedure in this ethnic group as follows:

"When death occurs, after burial, the chief will ask the relatives of the deceased man to list all the matrimonial property. After such listing, people disperse and meet again after 40 days. This is a memorial day that they call "kuphika alubaini". *Everybody disperses after the ceremony, they meet again after 10 days time at a ceremony called* "kugalausya maig'a". *At this ceremony,* nsudzulo *is conducted. Then all the property is brought outside for everybody to see. After it has been verified, distribution of the property is done by the widower, but if it is the husband who has died then distribution is done by his relatives."*

Though there would seem to be some variations in the procedures followed in these two tribes, the notable familiarity is that in both cultures the ceremony is used as a stage of property distribution and dispossession. While on the surface, it appears that it fosters amicable discussions, women are usually subjected to unfair distribution of property. The study revealed that the relatives of the deceased husband collect the matrimonial property of the couple during this ceremony by allotting a huge share of the property to themselves and leaving valueless items to the widow and children, regardless of entitlement. This was demonstrated in a case of one widow, Mrs. Chinangwa. She narrated that:

"During nsudzulo *ceremony, in the presence of the chief, the men's relatives and my relatives, my son and I were given only six plates and three gondolos (baskets that are used for picking tea). Yet as a family, we had two gardens of bananas, three houses and three gardens of tea. I was the one who was heavily involved and worked hard in the tea and banana gardens."*

Mrs. Chinangwa's case brings to light the extent to which social realities and daily practices of the people have a profound effect on widows despite any pronouncements in the law. Inheritance laws require fair distribution. It is important that the widow's entitlement needs to be settled before distribution is effected. *Nsudzulo* ceremony ignores this. Ncube and Stewart[46] correctly note that even where the law pronounces in the widows' favour, the realities that many of them face are very different because the practices of the community, the attitudes of the family and society create a different scenario. Widowhood becomes a situation where the woman is thrust into a new and often very problematic status. Not only is this status in conflict with her legal status, it is also the product of perceptions and actions of others and she herself may be a source through her own social perception and acculturation. Despite this anomaly, most of the men and women were of the view that the customs are fair. In Mulanje, interviewees were of the view that at least when custom is followed, and property is distributed during *'nsudzulo'*, people compromise. The reality, however, is that such compromise is based on genderisation. The widow is ultimately given what is viewed as feminine. In any case, the widow cannot sell crockery, since such items are necessities. The problem with genderisation is that the division is done without taking into account the widow's entitlement to the property. To the dispossessors, only *feminine* property can accrue to her. This means that she does not only get dispossessed of her share in her husband's property, but also the property that she owns in her own right. Further, the fact the chief does not automatically react to enforce the settlement of the widow's entitlement makes 'fairness' a fallacy.

The case of Mrs. Chinangwa shows that even the presence of the widow's relatives does not guarantee the immediate protection of the widow and her interests. The widow cannot express her dissatisfaction as she is 'bereaved.' If her relatives do not speak for her, she loses out. Normally, the relatives do not speak out because of the cultural mindset that once property is genderalised, then fair distribution has been achieved. Mrs. Chinangwa was partly helped by her son as:*"When my son in tears complained right there, he was given one half of the smallest garden."* Traditionally, the widow still had to submit her complaint to her *ankhoswe*. The *ankhoswe*, in turn would then take up the issue with the man's side and together to their village chief. In some cases such procedures can take a long period of time while the woman and her children are suffering. It cannot be expected that during this period the property is lying idle. By the time discussions take place, some of the property will have been wasted or outlived its usefulness. The immediate role of the chief in such circumstances is therefore uncertain. In the patrilineal South, a similar custom is known as *kudzimbula*.

5.4.3.2.2   During Kudzimbula
Kudzimbula is a customary practice prevailing amongst the Sena people. It is an indirect mode of property dispossession. *Kudzimbula* was described as a funeral ritual, whereby a widow is 'released' and escorted to live with her natal family in conformity with customary requirements. The practice takes place soon after her husband's death or at a later stage.

Female participants in a focus group discussion in Lunkhwe Village in Chikwawa District narrated that during the ritual, a widow is formally informed that she is free to re-marry. She is then given a nominal sum of money,[47] requested by her in-laws to pack her personal effects and is escorted back to her own family by his late husband's marriage advocate and other in-laws.

The *kudzimbula* ritual is a clear infringement of the widow's right not to be deprived of property, including that obtained by inheritance.[48] When leaving her matrimonial home, the widow is not entitled at custom to take any of the household property or matrimonial belongings. She does not have much say since the in-laws make all the decisions and her duty is to comply with them. During the research, the participants conceded that the customary practice is very unfair in excluding widows from taking a share in the household property. However, the female participants had been conditioned to the practice as part of their tradition and culture. *'Nanga munthu ungatani,'* was the common response, meaning *'what else can one do'*. This finding is similar to the observation made by the WLSA Zambia.[49] It was established in Zambia that social-cultural values and beliefs sometimes constrain women victims in their search for justice.

5.4.3.2.3   Abuse of Customs through Misinterpretation
When death occurs, some people take advantage of the situation and misinterpret customs prevailing in their societies to pave way for dispossessing the surviving spouse. In the matrilineal societies, such custom is *chikamwini*. In patrilineal societies, the custom is *lobola*.

i) Abuse of the Chikamwini Custom
The *chikamwini* custom is sometimes abused both against widowers and widows. The *chikamwini* arrangement is that the *mwini mbumba* is the

73

owner of the lineage. This includes his sisters and her children. The traditional implication of this is that the *mwini mbumba* has the sole responsibility of looking after these members of the extended family. On his part, a husband is also responsible for his own sisters' children. Notwithstanding this custom, modernization has seen to the shift of responsibilities, so that most fathers are now responsible for their nuclear families. The *chikamwini* custom is, however, often abused against the interest of widows. The custom makes some men believe that they have no legal duty to maintain their families. When the man dies, dispossession naturally follows because of the conviction that the children and widow cannot inherit the "property" of somebody who had no traditional duty to maintain them in his lifetime. The widow is expected to rely on her *mwini mbumba,* who has the ultimate responsibility to fend for the children. Her entitlement to the property is disregarded. Whatever may be left for the children and the wife is therefore the prerogative of the male side. It all depends on their goodwill. In situations where property dispossession occurs, the welfare of the children and the woman is not a matter of concern. If the children have been provided for, the woman naturally benefits indirectly as she is the custodian of the children. Some husbands, it was established, do not strongly accept their responsibility to maintain wives.

During a focus group discussion at Chitakale Tea Estate, it was clear that men put very little weight on their responsibility towards their wives and children. To most of them, marriage was clearly a medium of procreation, with no strings attached. Some men were loath of having their wives inherit their property to the extent that they were interested to know whether or not the law can support them if they left all the property acquired before marriage with their parents. Some men even wanted to know if inheritance laws would allow the wife to inherit even such property which, though acquired during marriage, had been kept away at their natal homes. They clearly were resentful to the thought that their wives could inherit their property at the expense of their parents or relatives.

On the other hand, the fact that marriages are matrilocal sometimes leads to the abuse of the *chikamwini* customs against widowers. Men expressed concern that the *chikamwini* custom is sometimes manipulated upon the death of the wife. One elderly man in Group Village Headman Namputu's area in Mulanje bitterly stated that:

"All the man's energy is spent at his wife's home and his investments are made there. But when the wife dies, her relatives sometimes dispatch the husband to his natal home with no or very little property. All the good things he might have been doing to make the life of his wife as well as her relatives comfortable are forgotten".

74

Further investigations revealed that the dispossession of widowers is very rare. It happens usually when the husband is elderly, and has no surviving strong kinsmen to support him. Otherwise, most of the widowers reported that they were still living in their late wives villages without any problem. The belief that all the property in the home belongs to a man and not to the wife protects most widowers from dispossession.

ii)   Abuse of Lobola Custom

Patrilineal societies follow the *lobola* custom whereby a woman lives at her husband's village. When the husband dies, the widow will still reside at his village. She will also continue using the matrimonial property, though she essentially does so as trustee for her children. Culturally, *lobola* entails that children belong to the husband's side. If she decides to leave her husband's home, she leaves both the property and the children behind. This custom is often abused since the wife's personal assets are also subsumed in her late husband's estate. In many cases, the children are viewed as the gates to the property, and therefore cases of dispossession in the patrilocal areas occur under the guise of practising the *lobola* custom, whereby both children and property get 'automatically' retained by the male side.

A male participant in Chief Lunkhwe's area in Chikwawa clearly elaborated that because the exchange of *lobola* implies that upon death of the husband, the children of the marriage become the responsibility of the deceased husband's relatives, relatives of the deceased man usually do not appreciate the need to share with the widow the matrimonial property because such property is supposed to devolve to the children. The husband's relatives are therefore afforded an opportunity to have access to the couple's matrimonial property in the name of tradition. Both male and female participants in the area admitted that the practice is quickly being overtaken by changing times and only happens in exceptional cases. Effective radio education programmes, which advocate against dispossession of widows, are contributing to the change. Previously, the widow would be dispatched to her natal family without property, except her own personal effects such as clothes. The widow was compelled to leave most of the household or matrimonial property behind, including kitchen utensils, supposedly for the use of the children of the marriage. In some areas, this continues to be the practice. In such cases, female participants revealed that if a widow insists on retaining physical custody of her children by taking them with her instead of subjecting them to the guardianship of the deceased's customary successor, she would still be deprived of household goods. This occurs although the dispossession is primarily done "for the children's sake." That just illustrates that mostly, dispossession is done to serve the interests of those dispossessing.

In some areas, the widow is allowed to retain kitchen utensils. During the general group discussions in the two districts visited in the Northern Region, the constructive nature of property dispossession arises due to the fact that a wife resides among her husband's clan. Once she decides to leave, she is to take only her pots and pans (*ziwiya*). The household goods such as tables and chairs are deemed to belong to the children who belong to the deceased husband's clan.

Widowhood devalues the woman's dignity and subjectivity. The construction of a wife's identity in the patrilineal societies does not seem to consider a wife as an individual in her own right. Accordingly, upon death of her husband, the widow's value to the clan depreciates. If she sometimes fails to comply with some of the elaborate funeral and mourning rituals, she may be chased out of her late husband's village. She therefore loses the household goods and custody of the children. This usually happens when the social relations are bad between the widow and her in-laws.

Many men strongly hold the views that the controller of property must be male. A group of twenty village leaders informed the researchers that household property belongs to the husband and not the wife. Upon death of the husband, the property transfers to the children of the marriage. The traditional leaders emphatically stated they would not intervene in the distribution of the household property even when the widow was their highly educated and high-income earning daughter. If, during the persistence of the marriage, the wife gives something to her parents, it is the duty of the parents to thank her husband (the son-in-law) who, is customarily, the assumed owner of the property. Should the husband pass away, then the widow's relatives would only be concerned with the loss of the son-in-law and mourn for him since they would have lost a source of support. They would not even consider that the man's property should benefit their daughter. This indicates that the widow is assumed not to have any interest in the matrimonial property. As such, she is constrained from seeking help from her people after being dispossessed. Such experiences and the cultural underpinnings are similar to those existing in Zambia,[50] where custom is also used as a scapegoat for dispossession.

Through the misinterpretations of customs both in the matrilineal and patrilineal societies, relations of a deceased person abuse such customs to dispossess the widow of both her own share in the estate and the property that exclusively belongs to her. This bears testimony to the fact that the issue of property dispossession appears to be guided by systems of custom, expectations, beliefs and assumptions that are rarely questioned and guide the behaviour of individuals in societies. This might be the case notwithstanding that such systems operate counter to statute laws of succession.[51]

5.4.3.2.4 *Levirate Unions/Widow Inheritance*
Dispossession of widows also takes place indirectly by inheriting the widow. Usually the deceased man's relatives inherit the wife and children with the intention of taking over control of the property for economic gains.

Among the patrilineal Tonga, the deceased man's family inherits the widow along with the property. This symbolises that the widow is also regarded as a material resource, together with the inanimate property. By virtue of their 'subordinate' status, women are assumed to have no property rights at all. Among the Tonga of Zambia,[52] on the death of her husband, the widow is given a levirate husband to take over her late husband's rights and duties. The widow continues to perform wifely duties to him in her deceased husband's village, thus remaining with her husband's property but without control. If, on the other hand, she opts to leave so as not to marry the levirate, she loses her access to her deceased husband's property. Where she opts not to marry the levirate and stays, her actions are closely followed and restricted up to a point where she cannot use some of the property without the consent of the deceased husband's relatives.

5.4.3.2.5 Institutional Dispossession

Dispossession of widows also indirectly takes place through institutional dispossession. For example where the district assembly office and the Administrator-General unfairly distribute death benefits. The district assembly distributes benefits by prescribing percentages to beneficiaries at their own discretion. The Administrator-General endorses such discretion by proceeding to disburse the benefits as advised. Mrs. Newa's case illustrates this experience.

When Mrs. Newa's husband died, the death benefits from his employers amounted to K77,000.00. The Administrator-General shared this sum between the widow, her four children, the deceased's mother, his two sisters and two brothers. The sum of K55, 000.00 was shared between the widow and four children. K22,000.00 was shared between the mother-in-law, the brothers and sisters. According to Mrs. Newa, the fact that the deceased terminal benefits had to be shared with his extended family relatives was unfair to her and children because it greatly reduced the share amounts that could be allotted to the children who needed financial assistance most. Her youngest child was only three months old when the father died.

The distribution was made to Mr. Newa's brothers and sisters notwithstanding that they had not been dependent on Mr. Newa during his lifetime. The allocation, further, was determined without any legal basis, occasioning injustice to the immediate family.

5.4.4 Causes of Property Dispossession

The research revealed that dispossession is caused by a number of social, cultural and legal factors. Most of them apply to both matrilineal and patrilineal societies. The predominant cause is the vulnerability of women, which is exacerbated when her husband dies. As her vulnerability increases, different vices, excuses, devices and plots are used to dispossess her. In many cases, the power vacuum left by the deceased husband is seized by his relatives to dispossess the widow, using a variety of methods.

5.4.4.1   Perceived Status of the Deceased

The economic status of the deceased relative to that of other relatives is one cause of property dispossession. This cause was identified in both matrilineal and patrilineal research sites. The participants narrated that the cases of dispossession are more common in situations where there is a reasonable amount of wealth in the family. Female participants explained that dispossession happens to 'wealthy' people. Malawi being one of the poorest countries, to the grassroots being wealthy is measured by the ownership of a lot of household assets and other 'luxuries' like a car, maize mill, grocery or other business, and any immovable asset. *Mrs. Sombeza*, a widow in Chief Fombe's area in Chikwawa, shared her story:

"At the time of my husband's death, we were living in a Blantyre location called Manase. We had two groceries, land and household assets. After my husband's burial at his village, I was never allowed to go back. A group of eighteen (18) people went to my house because, according to them, we were very wealthy and therefore had accumulated a lot of assets. They sold all the grocery stock and the plot of land. They only gave me one blanket and a mattress."

Even the case studies highlighted earlier in this chapter show that all the widows who were dispossessed had tangible assets. Some of widows and their families were clearly 'wealthy' by the standards of their husbands' relatives. In the case of *Mirriam Duwe*, she was dispossessed because she and her late husband had three minibuses, two pick-ups, one motorcycle and 70 corrugated iron sheets. In *Sarah Jalasi's* case, she and her late husband had a block of four houses and a grocery. *Mrs. Labana* was dispossessed of a commercial building and motor vehicles.

These cases highlight that relatives of the deceased man are reluctant to let the widow enjoy the 'wealth' on her own regardless of whether or not she contributed to its accumulation.

5.4.4.2   Lack of Children

Lack of children increases the widow's vulnerability to dispossession. In the patrilineal sectors inability to bear children within marriage is usually regarded as the wife's problem. Should the marriage subsist until death of the husband, this fertility problem is used to punish the widow by chasing her away from the man's home without any property. Where the matrimonial home is at a neutral place, the widow will often be dispossessed. The patriarchal stance is that the woman is not valued in her own right as an individual but as a good wife or bearer of many children. Should a woman fail to fulfill one of these roles, especially the latter, then she loses her womanhood and ought to be punished by those who have an interest in her reproductive roles. This state of affairs becomes even more prominent in that patrilineality endorses *maroworo* which, among other factors, signifies the transfer of the wife's reproductive and other rights to the man's side. However, if the wife does not bear children the clan's right to reproduce through her has been regrettably lost. Dispossession is hence a mode of punishment, in this regard.

Even in matrilineal societies, lack of children has been viewed as a legitimate ground for dispossessing the widow. In Mirriam Duwe's case, her *ankhoswe* reported that notwithstanding the fact that the property was jointly owned, he *lacked courage to approach his counterpart on the male side because he believed that the fact that Miriam had no children might jeopardise her chances of claiming any property.* This echoes Phiri's findings that historically, a woman's value in the matrilineal society was associated with having children.[53]

5.4.4.3   *Assertion of Male Dominance*
Dispossession occurs because male relatives want to assert their dominance over the widow. This is usually the case when the widow displays signs of independence. A practical example given in Chief Lunkhwe's area in Chikwawa was that sometimes during funeral arrangements, the widow's in-laws assume an authoritative and bossy roles, which the widow may not like. As such she may protest. Being offended by the widow's protests, disputes may arise between the widow and the in-laws that easily blow up and soon spill over to issues of property. The in-laws may then dispossess the widow just to emphasise on her 'subordinate' status. In the case of Mrs. Newa, who refused to stay in the village to look after her mother-in-law, the relatives took great offence to this and it was a contributory factor to her dispossession.

5.4.4.4   *Competition for Scarce Resources*
This study revealed that in most cases, widows are dispossessed of land and other scarce resources. In patrilineal societies, the underlying cause is the *lobola* marriage arrangement. Since the wife resides at her husband's village, normally the land that is used for gardening belongs to the husband's family. When the husband dies, the deceased person's relatives usually take the view that the widow has no right to continue using the land in question on her own since it ought to automatically revert to members of their family. The customary practice on succession to land takes precedence because the Wills and Inheritance Act does not apply to "customary land or to growing crops thereon".[54] Mrs. Mtize of Lunkhwe Village in Chikwawa District

was one of such victims when her husband of over 10 years died in 1999. She narrated that:

"My sister-in-laws deprived me of the garden that I had always used with my late husband. They argued that I had only been gardening there because it was my late husband who had the right to farm on the land. I needed the land to support my children and myself with food. Yet, my in-laws did not even have regard to the fact that due to the lobola *custom, the children were practically 'their' children and had a right to cultivate in their father's garden".*

Mrs. Veronica Bisenti, also of Lunkhwe Village, faced a similar experience, but her experience exemplifies that women can fight dispossession. She stated that *"When my husband died, my in-laws informed me that I could no longer use the gardens. However, I fought back and continued to use the gardens until eventually my in-laws left me alone. I just had to be stubborn and strong for the sake of my children, who need to be fed".*

In matrilineal societies, the widow is often dispossessed of land if the couple had acquired their own piece of land, independent of clan land. Traditional Authority Nthiramanja of Mulanje disclosed that most of his subjects are poor. The dispossession of land is therefore very common since it is the only tangible asset that can be a subject of dispossession. The only land that is spared is clan land and land acquired through chieftaincy. This latter land is always inherited by the successor to the chieftainship. However, the fact remains that the land is taken away from the widow's use.

These findings are a clear manifestation of competition for land, which is a scarce resource in Malawi. Women face stiff competition in acquiring land due to their lack of economic prowess and their position as the non-decision-maker both at family and community level. Due to the poverty situation, family members are willing to fight. In the end, it is only the fittest that survive and usually the women lose out.

5.4.4.5 *Insecurity over Competing Interests*
Most of the time, dispossession occurs because relatives of a deceased man get insecure with the widow's interest in her husband's estate. Usually, they feel the widow's interest will take precedence over their own. The relations therefore want to act swiftly before the widow's interest is determined, to serve their own interests. This is regardless of whether or not they are legally recognised dependants or heirs at customary law. Dispossession motivated by insecurity usually occurs soon after the death of a husband. Mrs. Dziko of T/A Nthilamanja's area in Mulanje narrated how the deceased's nephew harshly treated her:

"Soon after the death of my husband, his nephew, who never used to visit us while he was alive, demanded keys for the house. After three days, he told me that I am just a prostitute and I should go back to my village. I went back to my village with nothing, except my son. Yet we were married for 22 years. I was heart-broken but I could not do anything."

To protect their interests, relatives of the deceased man will do anything to disassociate themselves from the widows. This was revealed in Chief Lunkhwe's area in Chikwawa. Mrs. Bisenti's story was that:

"My in-laws demolished my house and destroyed all household items. This was to compel me to leave the village. My in-laws verbally harassed me and accused me of hanging around the marital village in the hope of benefiting from my deceased husband's death benefits. They considered my continued presence in their village as a threat to their interest in my deceased husband's death benefits. My presence was a constant reminder to them that as a widow, I was entitled to a share of the death benefits. They therefore knew that if I left the village, our relationship would be severed, and I would have no strong basis on which to claim a share of the death benefits. That way, they would obtain all the available money".

In the same village, Mrs. Mtize, also had her house nearly demolished by her in-laws. The plan was never carried out because she fought back.

" When they came and told me they wanted to demolish the house, I just stayed inside and kept my house locked and told them that if they wanted to demolish it, they would have to kill me inside as well. Eventually, they left me alone. They could not come back later in my absence because culturally, they are supposed to do it when I am there. Up to date, I am living in the same house though I have to farm far away in a garden that my parent's gave me after I had been dispossessed of the land by my sister-in-laws.

These incidents confirm other findings that even where the widow enjoyed good relationships with her in-laws, these may be denied so as to drive her out of the village.[55] Due to the high level of illiteracy and ignorance of the law among women, the widows do not even contemplate laying charges against their in-laws for their illegal, and sometimes criminal actions.

5.4.4.6   'Subordinate Status' Accorded to Women
One cross-cutting cause of dispossession is that most women do not control property, which is regarded as belonging to men. This entails that when a husband has died, the relatives assume that they have the right to take away from the wife and children the property that the family was using. The earning power of the woman is irrelevant. Even her own parents sometimes

refuse to acknowledge her as owner or controller of property. The woman, therefore, cannot receive much support from her own relatives.

5.4.4.7 Reaping from Human Capital and Investment

Another cross-cutting cause of dispossession is the belief that an investment was made in the deceased person from birth to marriage. Death provides the opportunity for realising the gains of such investment. Culturally, a child is 'owned and claimed' by all those who are related to him. Therefore, by virtue of being an uncle, brother, sister or parent of the deceased person, the relations feel that they have a major stake in 'his property' when he dies. The distributable form of such property is in the assets left after death. They further believe they have unequivocal power to distribute it.

5.4.4.8 Widow's Conduct

Almost all the men interviewed emphasised that the conduct of the wife is a strong determining factor in deciding whether or not to dispossess her. Conduct extended to the perceived neglect to look after the sick husband, as in the case of Mrs. Kulekana,

Mrs. Kulekana, who was a business woman, had continued to run her business of supplying fish to certain institutions during her husband's illness. The nature of the business demanded that she be away from home for several days, since she had to purchase the fish from Mangochi. Though she was doing this to make income for her family, to her in-laws, her conduct amounted to neglect of her husband's illness. When he died, they hurriedly dispossessed her on the ground that her conduct during illness had symbolized that she was a' prostitute' and did not care for her husband.

Conduct that may prompt dispossession also includes being seen in the company of other men either during the husband's illness or before *nsudzulo* (after the husband has died). Rudeness and hostility towards her in-laws during the subsistence of marriage is also unacceptable conduct for the in-laws. In Mulanje, even the conduct of the widow's relatives during her late husband's illness is monitored. During an interview held at Chitakale Tea Estate, one man elaborated the process of *conduct monitoring* by referring to an "invisible book."

"In a marriage situation, there exists an "invisible book". This book is mentally 'kept' by in-laws. It monitors all occurrences and notes down all the problems and faults. This becomes extensive during the husband's illness. During this time, the man's relatives record in the book all that is happening involving the wife and her relatives. This includes the conduct of the wife, the manner in which she is nursing her sick husband, whether any of her relatives quarreled during the time of sickness and whether or not the widow nursed her

sick husband all by herself or she sought the assistance of her in-laws. It is not acceptable to be assisted by in-laws in nursing the husband. Even where the in-laws have volunteered to do so, the wife is supposed to decline politely. If she accepts, it is misinterpreted as a sign that she is tired of nursing her husband. This may be used as a ground for dispossessing her of property.

This practice manifests the subordination of the woman whereby as women, they or their relatives are expected to behave in a particular way. Failure to do so results in dispossession as a punishment.

5.4.4.9 *Absence of a Will and Ignorance of the Law*

The research revealed that generally people do not leave wills. Very few individuals   leave some written document or word with some people. In most cases those documents and words are usually disregarded because people feel that they were manufactured by those placing reliance on such documents. In any case these 'wills' are not legally valid because they do not comply with the requirements under the Wills and Inheritance Act. The Act provides that a will has to be written and signed by the testator before two witnesses in the presence of each other.[56] Failure to follow this requirement makes the estate of a deceased person intestate. This gives a leeway to property dispossession, though the deceased person might have clearly intended to protect his family. Mrs. Labana, a widow from Mangochi Boma, was unfortunate to experience this.

Mrs. Labana's husband died in November 1999. At the time, the couple had amassed a lot of wealth including a nearly completed commercial building, two residential houses, a plot of land and three motor vehicles. They were also selling bricks. Before his death, Mr. Labana wrote a 'will' and deposited it at the district assembly. He distributed his assets amongst his wife and children. Unfortunately, the will only carried his signature and was invalidated by the court. His brother took advantage of this and took over the running of the family businesses. He ended up using the proceeds for his own ends. On some days, he would give the widow very little money to buy food for the week. According to Mrs. Labana, her brother-in-law was not taking care of her as he claimed, but she was being robbed. This is because as an individual, she already knew how to run the businesses herself since that was what she used to do with her husband. The amount of household money that her brother- in-law was giving her was far from adequate.

Mrs. Labana's misfortune was caused by ignorance of the law on the part of her husband. The district assembly also contributed to it because they failed to verify with late Mr. Labana on the validity of his 'will' before depositing it. The authority of his brother to manage the estate was further not supported by law, since he was not formally appointed as administrator.

83

5.4.4.10 Rebellion to 'Law'

In some instances, dispossession occurs as a sign of 'rebellion' against the 'existing' statute on inheritance. There is a general misconception in Mulanje District, for example, that under the Wills and Inheritance Act, the law is that all the property belongs to the wife and children. In an interview conducted at Chitakale Tea Estate in Mulanje, the men said they get such misconceived ideas from the district assembly. The assembly is said always to declare that in accordance with the law, all the property is to go to the wife and children. People are then reported to find such 'law' unacceptable and to dispossess the widow as a form of resistance. In fact, it was apparent that the interviewees were convinced that more often than not, because of this 'law', the widow is suspected of having deliberately killed her husband in order to inherit property. Consequently, she may be dispossessed on that ground.

The misconception seems to arise from the misinterpretation of 'household belongings', which the Act requires to be for the surviving wife's exclusive use.[57] In an interview conducted at the DC's office, it was clear that the phrase is misleading in that it is interpreted as meaning matrimonial property.

5.4.4.11   Deceit

Relatives sometimes use deceitful means to dispossess the widow. The cases where widows have been deceived show that widows are sometimes unsuspecting of their in-laws' true intention. They may therefore not invoke any remedies that are immediately available because they hope that matters will be sorted out sooner or later. Meanwhile, the in-laws use the property to their benefit. By the time the widows realise that they have been deceived, it may either be too late or they may have resigned to their fate as a result of giving up their rights to their property.

In Mrs. Labana's case, she narrated that she never intended to surrender her motor vehicles to her brother-in-law. However, her brother in-law deceived her that he needed the registration books and car keys for the vehicles to facilitate the change of registration numbers into new ones, according to government's demand. She never saw the assets again. When later she inquired, her brother-in-law retorted that the items were no business of hers. In Miriam Duwe's case when her father-in-law dumped her at the boma, she was told that she would be contacted at a later date to discuss distribution of property. By the time of the interview, her family had not complained to anybody because they were hopeful that Miriam's in-laws would carry out the promise of contacting them on a later date to discuss the distribution of the property; a thing that never happened and in the meantime Miriam was advised by her friends to be patient and wait for the invitation from the in-laws. Two years later, the invitation had not yet come. The property was still being enjoyed by the deceitful relatives.

The same was the situation in Mrs Chinangwa's case. In reaction to her in-laws' deceit, she said:

"To console me, the man's relatives said they would build me a house at home and yet a year has passed and nothing has been done. I was not satisfied with the way the property was distributed. I felt very bad and I was depressed. I have spent all my energies on those tea gardens and now I have nothing. My son is in Form Two and we have no source of support. At the moment we are waiting for a letter which my husband's relatives said they would write about the house. If the letter does not come I will go and see the DC."

Effects of Dispossession on Widows

The research revealed that dispossession of widows has social, economic and psychological effects.

5.4.5.1 Social Effects
Socially, dispossession normally leads to strained relations between the widow, children and the late husband's relations. In some instances, this becomes the last time that the two sides of the family will ever see each other again because their disagreements breed enmity. Like in the case of *Mrs. Yusufu*, after being duped of her share of her husband's death benefits, she decided to move to her natal area and start another life. Her relations with her in-laws were severed. Where dispossession has occurred widows tend to lose confidence in the extended family and the relationships with their in-laws are strained.

5.4.5.2 Economic Effects
Dispossession is logically deprivation. The interviewees explained that when dispossession occurs, women tend to suffer a lot because of the small economic base that they have. They are therefore left impoverished. In the words of Mirriam Duwe: *"Tangoganizirani kuti dzulo ndinali wolemera koma lero ndilibe chakudya kapena sopo yosambila"* (Just imagine that yesterday I was rich but today I do not have food to eat or soap for bathing). The findings show that the economic changes for widows can be quite drastic and can leave the widows in a lot of psychological pain that is difficult to come to terms with. The loss of the husband, who is often the perceived bread-winner, is economically devastating. The sudden loss of property and other resources leaves the widow and her children in a very vulnerable situation. The lifestyle changes at times to an unbearable situation. Where prop-

erty dispossession occurs, a widow is most often unable to support the family in terms of payment of rentals, school fees as well as purchasing of consumables. This leads to dependency on other family members, who already have their own responsibilities to take care of.[58]

5.4.5.3 *Psychological Effects*

Dispossession further leads to spirit injury. Dispossession disregards the widow's efforts. This demoralises her and kills or injures her spirit, as she is rendered helpless in the face of the society, family and justice. Women also lamented that they are like slaves who have just assisted in amassing property for others.

5.5 Conclusion

The findings have shown that dispossession of widows is a form of gender based violence. The widow is in a vulnerable position because of her status as a woman in society. Various processes of dispossession exploit and disempower her. These processes start with the socio-cultural dynamics of matrilineal and patrilineal societies as lineage patterns. These are structured to guarantee the wife's and widow's vulnerability. During marriage, property ownership is genderised in favour of men. The payment of *lobola* in patrilocal societies symbolises the transfer of the wife's reproductive and labour rights. She is therefore under the full control of her husband and kinsmen. A wife is perceived not to have any property rights, especially those relating to control. Everything in the matrimonial home belongs to the husband.

The death of a husband in both lineage patterns simply enhances the process of dispossession. This starts through the cultural bestowment of widowhood. This is important as it determines a 'widow's' right to inheritance. For a woman to qualify for the widowhood status, she has to fulfill certain marriage expectations. These include being of good conduct during the lifetime of her husband and even after his death. Further, her marriage ought to have been recognised at custom. When widowhood is bestowed, the widow is required to undergo abusive rituals, which in some cases are used to dispossess her of property.

The dispossession takes place in several stages. It also takes place directly and indirectly. Directly, dispossession may take place during the illness of the husband, bereavement and distribution of estates. Indirect dispossession occurs through the observance of rituals and customs such as *nsudzulo, kudzimbula, chikamwini* and *lobola*. The institutions established to handle estates of deceased person further aids the dispossession of widows.

The findings show that there are a number of causes of dispossession of widows. These include the perceived status of the widow, lack of children, assertion of male dominance, competition for scarce resources, insecurity over competing interests, low status accorded to women, reaping from human capital and investment, widow's conduct, absence of a will and ignorance of the law, rebellion to 'law', and deceit. Finally, the effects of dispossession are against the rights of the widow as a woman. As a result of property dispossession, the widow loses socially, psychologically and economically. In many cases, the widow is unable to recover and is thrust into a cycle of deprivation manifested through poverty, emotional misery, and shortage of choices. When faced with such situations, most widows go to search for justice at various structures of justice delivery. The next chapter will show how these structures respond to the issue of dispossession.

---

[1] Ibik J.O (1970), p79.

[2] Kasman E., and Chirwa,C,(1997

[3] Phiri I.A, (1997).

[4] Ibid, p.32

[5] Phiri K.M, (1983) p.259.

[6] Mbiti J. S, (1987) p.7.

[7] Phiri, I.A., (1997 p. 37

[8] Phiri, ibid.

[9] Among the patrilineal Tonga, who practise *chihara.*

[10] In 2000, the sum paid for *Luphatho* was K50.00

[11] In 2000, this figure was between K500.00 and K1, 000.00
[12] Section 22 (5) of the Constitution of Malawi

[13] A neutral place is an area where none of the spouses originally come from. It has no attachments of kinship to either, whether by affinity or consanguinity.
[14] April 2000

[15] Kanyongolo, F., (July 2000)

[16] ibid.

[17] WLSA Mozambique, (1996), p.60.

[18] Section (24)(b)(i) of the Constitution

[19] Section (24)(2)(c), ibid

[20] Section (24)(1)(ii), ibid

[21] Section 5 of the Constitution

[22] Section 16 & of the Wills and Inheritance Act, which recognize a wife as one of the beneficiaries to the estate of a deceased man.

87

[23] WLSA Zimbabwe

[24] WLSA Swaziland, (1998) p.139.

[25] Section 24(1)(a)(ii)

[26] Nkhoma and Kirwan, (1996).

[27] WLSA Malawi (2000) pp46-47.

[28] WLSA Zambia (1994)

[29] Dow, U., and Kidd. P.,(1994) p92

[30] Ibid,88

[31] Section 22 (5)

[32] Ncube W. and Stewart J(eds.). (1995) p. 36.

[33] WLSA Zambia (1994)

[34] Speech delivered by Honourable Samuel Kandodo Banda, then Chair of the Legal Affairs Committee of Parliament, at the launch of the White Scarf Campaign during the 16 days of Activism Against Violence Against Women, (25th November 2000).

[35] Dow, U., and Kidd, P. supra,.(1994), 77-78.

[36] Amadiume, I., (1987) p.83

[37] Ncube W. and Stewart J(eds.). (1995) p 34.

[38] Amadiume, I., (1987), *Gender and Sex in an African Society*, Zed Books Ltd, London.p.81

[39] WLSA Zambia, (1997) p.184

[40] ibid

[41] under Section 5.4.3.2

[42] WLSA Zambia (1994)

[43] Section 42, Wills and Inheritance Act (Cap 10:02), Laws of Malawi.

[44] Section 25, ibid.

[45] Story appears in Chapter Six.

[46] Ncube and Stewart (eds), (1995) p. 36.

[47] In 2000, the figure was 20 tambala.

[48] Section 24(2) (c) of the Republican Constitution

[49] WLSA Zambia (1994)

[50] WLSA Zambia (1994)

[51] WLSA Zambia, (1994),supra

[52] WLSA Zambia, (1994),supra

[53] Phiri, I.A., (1997) p.33

[54] Section 1 (3) of the Act

[55] WLSA Zambia, (1997) p.184

[56] Section 5 (1)

[57] Section 17 (1) (b)

[58] Sakala F., (1998), p.46.

Chapter Six
THE WIDOW IN SEARCH OF JUSTICE

6.1 Introduction

The previous chapter has shown how the process of dispossessing a widow occurs and how it infringes upon a widow's rights to property in different ways and for diverse reasons. This chapter discusses the type of redress available through the justice delivery structures to a dispossessed widow. The argument being made in this chapter is that only a few of the justice delivery structures are accessible to dispossessed widows.

6.2 Justice Delivery Structures in Malawi

The several justice delivery structures where women may access justice have been classified into traditional and central, support institutions[1]. Traditional structures like marriage counsellors, chiefs and churches are the structures that are most accessible to a woman in search of justice. The central structures are those provided by the legal system that include the judiciary, the police, the office of the district assembly and the Administrator-General. The support institutions are hospitals, the church, social welfare and human rights non-governmental organizations. The traditional family structures where a widow seeks redress are *ankhoswe* and the chief. The central structures that are directly connected with inheritance law and succession are the offices of the district assembly, the Administrator-General and the courts. The central structure that is indirectly connected with administering deceased estates is the Office of the Ombudsman. The support structures are the social welfare office and non-governmental organisations.

6.3 *Ankhoswe* and Dispossessed Widows

The research findings show that some dispossessed widows who seek redress ordinarily complain to the justice delivery structures that are easily accessible to them such as the *ankhoswe* and the chief. When the dispute fails to be resolved at these levels, it goes to the offices of the district assemblies, social welfare office, non-governmental organizations and in very rare circumstances the court and the ombudsman[2].

The family system as a dispute resolution mechanism is problematic because of the role of the *ankhoswe*. The *ankhoswe* are supposed to be counsellors of the husband and wife during the subsistence of their marriage[3]. When a husband dies, the role of guardianship of the widow is assumed by the *mwini-mbumba* in matrilineal societies and the husband's clan in patrilineal societies. Sometimes the *mwini-mbumba* (who may also be the *ankhoswe*) for the deceased husband can also violate the widow's rights to property by dispossessing her entitlement to household belongings. The *mwini-mbumba* during this period holds the view that he has to be the custodian of property that belonged to, for instance, his deceased nephew.

The *ankhoswe* and other customary heirs from a deceased man's clan often fail to address issues of the widow's entitlement rights to the property as provided for her by the Wills and Inheritance Act and act illegally by assuming powers of administration. In addition, under customary law in matrilineal societies, the deceased father's clan is not responsible for maintenance of children of a marriage[4]. Consequently, dispossessing a mother of property may have detrimental effects on the lives of children of the marriage. The failure of the *ankhoswe* for the widow to assert the widow's property rights in the estate of her husband implies that the *ankhoswe* have breached their customary duty of defending and protecting her against outsiders. On the other hand, although the *ankhoswe* of the deceased man are customarily required to ensure that the estate is distributed to nieces and nephews, it is asserted that the *ankhoswe* can only do this once the issues of entitlement under the Wills and Inheritance Act have been resolved. If anything the *ankhoswe* should only exercise control over the share for customary heirs and should not allow a conflict between the *ankhoswe* himself as beneficiaries and as marriage advocates.

The research found that some *ankhoswe* for the widow fail to assist a dispossessed widow because they are ignorant of the statutory law on inheritance and succession or some prejudices that they harbour about women's roles. As was discussed in the previous chapter, childlessness is a factor that can cause a widow being dispossessed of property. In addition, the emotional distress of a widow affects the amount of effort that she puts in asserting for her rights to property. This is illustrated by the case of a young widow, Miriam Duwe, from Traditional Authority Jalasi in Mangochi District.

Miriam Duwe and her husband, during their ten years of marriage, operated mini-bus transport services in and around Mangochi District.

90

Shaibu Kabichi, Miriam's *ankhoswe* and *mwini mbumba*, felt disrespected and perturbed by this act of "dumping" her at the boma and not escorting her to her village. Shaibu Kabichi stated that Miriam's father-in-law deliberately did this because he "was afraid that if he came to my house I would demand that they distribute the property". However, Miriam and her *ankhoswe* did not seek redress from any justice delivery structure because they were optimistic that the father-in-law would fulfill his promise and call for a meeting to distribute the property. Further, the ankhoswe failed to take further action to assert Miriam's property rights due to ignorance of the statute law. The father-in-law's action was illegal since all administrators and receivers of estates are supposed to be appointed by a court of law.

Miriam claimed that she was greatly aggrieved by her husband's death and that it was emotionally difficult for her to discuss the distribution of the property. Shaibu Kabichi, her *ankhoswe*, stated that he lacked courage to approach his counterpart on the male side because he believed that the fact that Miriam did not bear any children with the deceased person might jeopardize her chances of claiming any interest in the estate of her husband.

6.4 Chiefs and Dispossessed Widows

Chiefs are important when a widow is going through the ritual of *nsudzulo* or *kumeta* in both patrilineal system and matrilineal marriage systems. The role of the chief is to facilitate fair distribution and play a mediatory role. The research found that a widow raises misgivings about distribution only after the distribution ceremony. She has to raise her objections only through her *ankhoswe* who represent her before the *ankhoswe* for the deceased husband. A family conference is usually attended by the *ankhoswe* and traditional leaders such as the chiefs, who mediate on contentious issues.

In some cases some chiefs do not play an active role in terms of assisting women to assert their legal rights when property is being distributed. This is illustrated by the case of Mrs. Chinangwa from Mulanje District, who stated that during the *nsudzulo* ceremony in the presence of the chief as well as her relatives, the deceased husband's relatives only gave her six plates and three *gondolos*[5]. The deceased man's relatives dispossessed her of two gardens of bananas, three houses, three gardens for growing tea as well as most household belongings.

In most cases the chiefs emphasise on contact and dialogue to ensure that there is fair distribution of the estate. For example, in Sara Gulani's case, Village Headman Chowe of Traditional Authority Jalasi, assisted a dispossessed widow by ensuring that Village Headman Kachere of Blantyre convened a family conference to discuss the distribution of the matrimonial property. At the meeting the chief proceeded to distribute the houses and groceries in dispute between the widow and her brother-in-law. However, the brother-in-law never permitted Sara Gulani to occupy the houses in Kachere Township or receive rentals from them.

The limitations encountered by the chiefs in assisting dispossessed widows are that most chiefs are not fully aware of principles governing distribution of deceased persons estates as stipulated by statutory law. Most chiefs believe that fair distribution is achieved by considering factors such as the existence of children in the family, the need to care for surviving parents and other humane considerations. Although the chiefs appreciate their role and responsibility in the resolution of disputes related to property dispossession, their authority and capacity to do so is limited. Firstly, chiefs are not legally allowed to appoint themselves as administrators. Secondly, if they do act as administrators of an estate their orders are not enforceable. Thirdly, some chiefs can also be biased against dispossessed widows or be bribed by influential perpetrators of property dispossession.

6.5 District Assemblies and Dispossessed Widows

Due to the difficulties experienced by traditional leaders in enforcing orders, chiefs usually refer a dispossessed widow to higher authorities such as the district assembly. The Wills and Inheritance Act[6] provides that district assemblies should distribute institutional monies in deceased estate if the sum does not exceed K20, 000.00[7]. The study found that property dispossession cases are some of the important women's rights issues that this offices handles[8].

When district assembly officers are settling matters pertaining to deceased persons' estates, traditional leaders are usually requested to be present. The reason is that the chiefs are expected to help with the parties compliance with orders made by the district assembly. The case of Maureen Nyemba of Bereu Village in Chikwawa District illustrates how the office of district assembly coordinates with other justice delivery structures such as chiefs, the Administrator-General and NGOs in the course of assisting widows to attain justice.

When Maureen Nyemba's husband passed away, she was in possession of property that included six houses, a maize mill, two grocery shops and about K30,000.00 in the deceased's bank account. Maureen's father-in-law disliked the idea of Maureen operating the matrimonial businesses at Bereu Trading Centre and demanded that she vacates the matrimonial home, which was behind the two groceries. The chiefs were unable to resolve the conflict between the relatives of Maureen's husband and herself and the matter was referred to Chikwawa District Assembly. The District Commissioner in the presence of the traditional leaders ordered that the widow and her children continue to reside behind the grocery and operate the shop. On their return to Bereu, Maureen's father-in-law and brother-in-law threatened the chiefs who thereafter desisted from monitoring the father-in-law's compliance with the orders of the chief executive. Subsequently, Maureen was badly assaulted by her brother-in-law because he was angered that the grocery and matrimonial home had been given to her by the District Commissioner. The father-in-law locked the shops and kept the keys. The chief could not assist the widow. Since the chief did not take any action to address the problem Maureen filed a complaint with the police. The police threatened the offending parties with prosecution. Eventually, the District Commissioner referred the matter to the Administrator-General and Malawi CARER, a non-government organisation.

6.5.1 The Practice of Clerical Officers

District assembly clerical officers through mediation resolve cases involving widows. If the arbitrator is convinced that the widow has been dispossessed of household belongings, he/she rules in favour of the widow and proposes a fair distribution of the property. Children are allocated a higher share of the institutional money than the wife followed by customary heirs. However, the half and half or two fifths and three fifths formulas are not strictly applied. In some cases the clerical officers also distribute household goods and other moveable property as if they are estate administrators. In distributing the property, preference is given to the deceased man's immediate family. Relatives of the deceased man are given a share because they are assumed to have been dependant on the deceased person. One reason is to avoid creating enmity between the widow and the deceased man's relatives who usually regard the deceased person's property as belonging to their late *mwini-mbumba*.

The research found that district assemblies are easily accessible to dispossessed widows in that they are able to act quickly when called upon and most people respect the decisions that the assemblies reach. For example, the clerks of district assemblies assist dispossessed widows to physically reclaim their property. In Blantyre, a widow complained at the district assembly of threats of being dispossessed of houses in Che Mussa, Blantyre, by relatives of the deceased. The matter was resolved when officers visited the plot to negotiate with the relatives to let the widow occupy one of the three houses, the mother-in-law one house while the third house was rented out.

Although district assemblies dispense justice, the research found out that some district assemblies act beyond their legal powers in their methods of settling property disputes. In as much as the district assembly could assist the Administrator-General to determine value of an estate by visiting the widow's matrimonial home, it is unlawful for them to distribute the unliquidated part of estate. Some district assemblies acknowledged that they are not legally mandated to distribute deceased persons' estates without letters of administration. Such assemblies referred matters to the Administrator-General's office.

In any case, relatives of a deceased man rarely obey orders by the district assembly. The case of Ziyaya illustrates this point. In this case, a grandfather refused to share the household property with his grandchildren as ordered by the Mchinji District Assembly. His response was that: *"Zivute zitani katundu sangachoke m'nyumba mwanga"* (No matter what happens the property will not leave my house). However, he later did give some of the electronic appliances (small fridge, hotplate, radio) and two bicycles to the children while the majority of the goods were sold at give away prices. For example, he sold a deep freezer that had cost the couple K15, 000.00 at K1,500.00.

6.5.2. Administration of Estates

The district assemblies assist the Administrator-General in determining the amounts of benefits to be awarded to beneficiaries. The system involves distributing the property based on the age pro rata basis whereby the younger the child, the higher the percentage. A share is also divided among the relatives of the deceased husband and widow. In two cases, the institutional funds were distributed as follows:

Blantyre District Assembly
Mrs. Banda's case

Mother	25%
Widow	20%
Daughter 5 years	30%
Brother 24years	9%
Brother 26years	8%
Brother 22years	8%

In the above case, half of the money was given to the wife and children, the other half went to the deceased mother and brothers of the deceased person. There were no indications on file as to whether the brothers were dependent on the deceased person or that they were customary heirs. It was not even clear how the percentage shares were arrived at.

Mzuzu District Assembly
Mrs. Newa's Case

Total benefit	=	K77, 000.00
Baby (3 months)	=	K15, 000.00
Other children between 1 – 12years = K11, 000 x 3 =		K33, 000.00
Widow	=	K 7,000.00

94

A K45, 000. 00 balance was divided between mother of the deceased, two sisters and two brothers of the deceased.

The principles of fair distribution state that in patrilineal areas one half of the estate will be distributed to the widow and children while the remaining half will be distributed to heirs at customary law. According to the principles of fair distribution of intestate estates for patrilineal areas the institutional funds should have been distributed based on levels of beneficiary dependency. Since children and a widow have different levels of dependency on the deceased man their shares should be different. In addition, the widow is entitled to the household belongings.

In the six research districts, the district assemblies in practice did not have an exact formula to determine the shares. When requested to explain how they had arrived at the percentages the clerks stated that: "It is how things are done around here." In Nkhata Bay District the clerks indicated that: "We just work *mwachimbulimbuli*" (literally meaning "in ignorance"). The study also found that district assemblies do not seem to regard the widow as one of the primary beneficiaries. In some cases she is considered to have the same degree of dependency as relatives of the deceased man. Consequently administrative structures that are supposed to deliver justice such as District Assemblies facilitate the deprivation of widow's entitlements. In that, part of the widow's entitlement is allocated to the relatives.

6.6 The Administrator-General: A Public Office in Chaos

The office of the Administrator-General is a body corporate established under the Administrator General Act[9]. In practice, however, it is a department within the Ministry of Justice headed by the Attorney-General. The mandate of the office of the Administrator-General is to protect the property of a deceased by applying to the High Court for letters of administration[10]. Any person can also appoint the Administrator- General to be executor of his or her will. There is only one office in Malawi which is located in Blantyre.

6.6.1 The Role of the Administrator-General
The office of the Administrator-General is physically located in Blantyre City. The role of the office is to administer deceased estates and to arbitrate in cases where district assembly chief executives have failed to mediate[11]. Where the complainants are not satisfied with the decision of the Administrator-General's office, an appeal lies to the High Court[12].

A widow's complaint about property dispossession is arbitrated by examining officers and assistants through a process of negotiation. The research established that the office delegates the responsibility of identifying beneficiaries to district assemblies, but without guidelines. As administrators of the estate, they can order relatives of a deceased man to comply with the provisions of the Wills and Inheritance Act and return all the household goods to a dispossessed widow. Moveable goods other than household goods are distributed by way of agreement among disputing parties. The office may approve the agreement by the widow and relatives of a deceased man. The case of Mr. Phiri's estate illustrates this practise. Mrs. Phiri, the widow, lodged a complaint of mismanagement of her deceased husband's estate by her stepson. The estate comprised of houses, motor vehicles and farmland. The office of the Administrator-General advised the widow and the stepson to discuss how they wanted the estate to be distributed and inform the office of their views. After the administrator had examined their consent agreement, he endorsed it and the property was distributed accordingly.

In some cases where disputing parties cannot reach a compromise, the office refers the case to the office of the Director of Public Prosecutions (the DPP). At the time of the research, the Administrator-General's office had referred three cases to the DPP's office but the outcome was not yet known because the DPP had referred the matter further to the police for investigations.

6.6.2 Problems Encountered
The office of the Administrator-General has procedural and capacity related problems.

6.6.2.1 Procedural Problems
The procedures to ascertain and establish the identity of beneficiaries can be subject to fraud. Some dispossessed widows lack proper identity documents such as a passport or employee identity card, yet these documents are required by the office. In some cases, however, benefits are allocated without ascertaining that all submitted names of beneficiaries are genuine. Sometimes relatives of a deceased husband may conspire to exclude the widow. A relative may bring a different person to impersonate the widow or child. The case of Ethel Yusuf discussed in chapter five illustrates that such procedures are prone to fraud.

A related problem is the office's failure to contact beneficiaries about impending administration. As a result most files lie dormant in filing cabinets. Work on files is activated when beneficiaries make an inquiry. Those potential beneficiaries who do not make such inquiries face the risk of being dispossessed. Although the Act provides that unclaimed funds or small balances should be published in the government *gazette* the office does not issue such notices. In any case most people do not have access to the *Gazette*. Further, the office does not seem to comply with the provisions of the Act[13] and when they attempt to do so, the processes are slow.

As they deal with widows the public officers rarely provide timely or accurate information. In addition, the dignity of the widow is rarely respected as she is subject to rudeness and neglect.

Mrs. Sherry Ziyaya is a copy typist whose ex-husband passed away in February 1999, leaving her with four children. The death gratuity of the deceased civil servant was sent to the Administrator-General in August 2000 and amounted to almost K120,000.00. When Mrs. Ziyaya visited the offices to check on the benefits she was told to check at the New Building Society Bank. She visited the bank five times on different days and on all those occasions returned to report that the deceased's money had not been deposited there. Further, the officers were rude and intimidating. The officers never explained to her the procedures involved. As Mrs. Ziyaya put it: "Mayankhindwe ake amakhala motikalipira kapena kutiwopseza" *(literally meaning "the responses from the officers were often harsh or meant to intimidate us"). For example, when she wanted information the officer told her to place her file on the officer's desk and wait on the bench in the corridor. In the end she lost confidence in the office and suspected that the officers had misappropriated the benefits:* "Mwina ndalama zinagwiritsidwa ntchito koma sakufuna kutiuza chilungamo".

Another case illustrating mismanagement of estates is that of Rachel Mwanja. Rachel Mwanja went to the Administrator-General to collect money on behalf of herself and her widowed mother who was staying in Karonga. Her father passed away in 1998. When she reported at the Administrator-General's office she was told that there was need to add more beneficiaries to include relatives. The office told her to send a fax to the Chief Executive of Karonga District Assembly that her relatives should submit names of other beneficiaries. The total value of the institutional money was about K80,000.00. To her surprise the money got reduced to K71,000.00 - the office claiming to have used some of the money to maintain a book balance, high court fees, government forms, Administrator-General's forms and tax arrears. In the process of trying to get her and her mother's entitlements, Rachel lost money through accommodation, transport, communication and other incidental costs. When she was eventually informed that the cheque had been drafted it was discovered that her file had been forgotten at one of the officer's home who was unwell and had to work at home. That resulted in further delays for her to return home, more than 600 kilometres away.

6.6.2.2. Inadequate Human and Financial Resources
The Administrator-General's office is greatly understaffed. Of the 44 established posts only 16 were occupied at the time of this research. A majority of the held posts were for junior staff. The personnel composition adversely

affects the efficiency of the office and quality of work. The understaffing also encourages corruption and bribery in the office that at one time resulted in the interdiction of several clerical officers who had mismanaged estates of deceased persons in 1999. Clerical officers with no training in accounts were working in the accounts departments.

Financially, the office is supposed to get K13 million per year. However, at the time of research, only K6,300.00 per month from the Treasury Cashier was being allocated to it. Such a small allocation affects the running of the office. When researchers visited the office, it was found out that there were no electricity and water utilities because these had been disconnected due to unsettled bills. The telephones services had just been reconnected. Furthermore, the office lacks computers that could be used for keeping vital information and for speedy processing of claims. The examining officers explained that sometimes client's files are taken away by the clients themselves and cannot be traced. Sometimes the files are misplaced within the office and it delays the process of assisting clients. One afternoon during the research, one of the assistants did not return from lunch in good time. Since he had left his office open, frustrated clients walked into the office and collected their files hoping to be helped by another examining officer.

6.7 The Ombudsman and Dispossessed Widows

The Ombudsman's office may only deal with property dispossession complaints against the conduct of any public office and there is no other court remedy available. Section 28 of the Constitution of Malawi provides that every person has the power to acquire property alone or in unison with others and that no person shall be arbitrarily deprived of property. This section read together with Section 15(2) of the constitution, provides the Ombudsman with the authority to investigate and determine issues of property dispossession. Section 15(2) provides that any person having sufficient interest in the protection of human rights in the Constitution is entitled to relief including from the Ombudsman. Further, by virtue of Section 123 of the constitution, the Ombudsman is empowered to investigate any and all cases where a person feels he or she has suffered injustice and there does not appear to be any remedy through the courts. Also Section 5 of the Ombudsman Act gives the Ombudsman powers to investigate any complaint including complaints of property dispossession as long as it involves maladministration of a public office. In the case of *Che Mbotere Mangwaya*, the mother of a deceased man filed a complaint against the Administrator-General that his delays in administering the estate had resulted in property dispossession by some of the children of the deceased. The Ombudsman ordered the Administrator-General to administer the case quickly and that the dispossessors should account for the property they had wasted.

When a complaint is lodged, discussions are organised in order to reach an amicable solution. Where the respondent does not respond or the discussions are unsuccessful, the matter is referred to the Ombudsman for determination through a mini-trial. Mostly the office receives complaints of maladministration of deceased estates against the Administrator-General and the district assembly offices. In the case of complaints against the Administrator-General's office, the clerks and the Ombudsman have tried to mediate so as to reach a settlement.

6.8 Social Welfare Office: Counselling Dispossessed Widows

The study found that some dispossessed widows seek redress from the social welfare office. Such cases mainly involve orphans. Discussions with social welfare officials revealed that their main role is the provision of counselling services and acting as a link between the affected widow and children and their village chief. They do not in any way adjudicate over property dispossession cases. Their main interest is on the psycho-social aspects of property dispossession.

When an issue is reported to social welfare officers, they carry out 'social investigation', to find out the background of the widow, which include her family background, how the marriage was celebrated and who was contributing towards the family income. After these investigations are through, the welfare officers hand over the case to a village chief with advice on how such a case could be resolved. If the case does not need to go the chief, they refer the victim to any office that they deem appropriate to handle the matter.

Although these officers do not play any adjudicatory role, the work they do in providing counselling and information is commendable. It has been noted that apart from economic deprivation, property dispossession also affects widows and children psychologically. The social welfare offices have staff who are appropriately trained to handle such issues. However, the officers were of the view that the other structures that deal with property dispossession do not clearly recognise this counselling role. Instead, the work of the officers is viewed as interference.

6.9 Courts and Dispossessed Widows

Although the Wills and Inheritance (Amendment) Act outlaws property dispossession, an examination of the types of cases filed with courts shows that very few property dispossession cases are filed with the courts. A magistrate in Blantyre reported that he had never presided over a case of property dispossession. One magistrate in Mzuzu had only heard one case of property dispossession over the past two years. This particular trial was prosecuted by the DPP himself since in the words of one of the magistrates "the police prosecutors do not seem to know that property dispossession is a criminal offence".

Although the Courts Act does not authorize a magistrate to distribute property, the courts are involved in issues to pertaining to estate administration in the process of distributing institutional funds. In Blantyre, the magistrate explained that issues of deceased person estates that are brought before the court as being only limited to examination of forms issued by the district assembly on distribution of money. The role of the magistrate in such instance is to ensure that the beneficiaries of the estate are ascertained correctly. This means that the magistrate has to confirm that the distribution is made in accordance with the provisions of the Wills and Inheritance Act.

The magistrates courts also recognise that property dispossession is a serious problem and it would have been proper if the magistrates were given the mandate to actually adjudicate over property distribution, rather than leaving such mandate with the district assembly's office as is currently the case. The magistrates suggested that the judiciary could consider setting down rules for property distribution and make it a judicial issue because most of the officers who currently deal with such issues in the district assembly's office and Administrator-General's issues are not competent enough to handle matters pertaining to estate administration. If the magistrates handled such matters they would be making the judicial services more accessible to the rural majority who are subject to property dispossession.

6.10 Civic Organisations and Dispossessed Widows

The study also found that some NGOs handle issues of property dispossession. At Malawi CARER most of the cases on property dispossession were brought by women. An average of eight women seek assistance on property issues every week. The organization has paralegals whose duty is to mediate. Complicated cases are referred to legal officers. The legal officers may pursue litigation if mediation fails.

The legal officers narrated a case in which a husband had committed suicide and left property but no will. After the funeral, the deceased man's relatives took the keys for one of the houses on grounds that the widow was to blame for the death. The uncle of the deceased was in the forefront of grabbing the property. Malawi CARER obtained an injunction and the uncle refused personal service of the order and did not comply with it. When the office sought to commence committal proceedings against the perpetrator, the court file could not be traced and the widow suspected that the perpetrator was behind the disappearance.

In *Susan Labana's case*, WLSA assisted Mrs. Labana to apply for letters of administration and obtained an interlocutory injunction against the brother of the deceased husband who was wasting the estate. The organisation and the legal practitioner for the brother-in-law later agreed to prepare a consent order on the property distribution.

6.11 Other Constraints to Seeking Justice

The research revealed that some dispossessed widows may not attempt to seek redress from the formal structures for fear that they might be bewitched. Consequently, a dispossessed widow is bound to lose her entitlements if the informal structures do not provide her with adequate relief. Alwan's[14] study shows that witchcraft is another setback to eradicating property dispossession in Malawi. Alwan's[15] study found that some widows are reluctant to take legal action when they experience property dispossession due to the fear of witchcraft upon themselves and their children. Similarly, this study found that the fear of witchcraft is one of reasons for not reporting incidences of property dispossession. A group of Lomwe women interviewed in Mulanje stated that most widows whose property has been dispossessed fear seeking redress due to the utterance of words such as *"tiona"* (literally meaning "we will see"), *"upita"* (literally meaning "you will go") which connote that acts of witchcraft can befall a complainant of property dispossession. These words are intended to threaten or intimidate a dispossessed widow from asserting her rights to the objects of property that may form part of her deceased husband's estate.

6.12 Conclusion

The research findings reveal that a dispossessed widow has problems obtaining redress from most of the justice delivery structures. The *ankhoswe* and chief sometimes fail to assist a dispossessed widow by their failure to timely assert for the widow's property rights. The dispossessed widow in her search for social justice finds that some of the central structures are constrained in delivering justice to her due to procedural problems and inadequate human and financial resources. However, support institution such as NGOs are complementing the traditional family structures and central structures efforts to assist dispossessed widows.

---

1 WLSA Malawi, (2000) p26

2 WLSA Malawi, (2000)

[3] see WLSA Malawi, (2000) p.27

[4] Phiri, I.A. (1997) p. 116

[5] Baskets used for picking tea

[6] Section 63

[7] Section 63(2)

[8] WLSA Malawi (2000) p. 42

[9] Section 2. chapter 10:01 of the Laws of Malawi

[10] Section 6 of the Act

[11] WLSA Malawi (2000) p. 48

[12] WLSA Malawi (2000) p. 48

[13] Section 11

[14] Alwan,(1997

[15] Alwan,(1997)

Chapter Seven

RECOMMENDATIONS

In the light of the research findings the study recommends that the following issues be taken into consideration if widows are to be protected from property dispossession:

7.1   It is clear that the process of dispossessing the widow starts at marriage. The decision by a woman to enter into a matrimonial set-up is not well protected by the law. This mainly refers to ownership of matrimonial property. The current marriage regimes are silent on the issue. It is therefore recommended that the Law Commission through its programme in reviewing gender-related laws should review all laws relating to marriage. Further the legislators should consider the approaches that are employed in other jurisdictions whereby marriage statutes clearly define property rights (regimes) between husband and wife. The Malawi Marriage Act does not specifically provide for property regimes in marriage upon the celebration of the same. It would therefore be imperative that marriages at custom should also be subject to property regimes, which would eventually protect spouses at death.

In this regard caution must be taken in the light of the words of the Constitution which state that women are entitled to property at divorce which is "jointly" owned. It is difficult to qualify what 'jointly' might mean in the light of the Marriage Act and in the true meaning of the words of the Constitution. This would therefore be one of the issues that need to be ironed out by legislators.

It is further recommended that all forms of marriage, whether traditional or otherwise be harmonised into one statute that looks at the property rights within these marriage regimes. The distribution of property should be based on principle of equity, rights and fairness by looking at both financial and non-financial contribution by both spouses.

7.2   The laws of intestacy under the Wills and Inheritance Act do not conform to the current democratic and moral theory. They are outdated and ambiguous, their existence have caused hardship to many especially widows. The Wills and Inheritance Act must be repealed in its entirety. A new law based on the current democratic and moral theory of equality, rights, justice and fairness must be put in place. The Law Commission under the gender-related laws programme should prioritize this issue. The research work that was done by the Core Group on the Wills and Inheritance Act on the Knowledge, Attitudes and Practices on the wills and Inheritance issues will be helpful.

7.3   It is further clear that magistrate courts have a larger role to play in protecting widows from property dispossession. The rules of procedure should give greater powers to magistrates in dealing with civil remedies such as injunctions or interim letters of administration.

7.4   Regard must be had to the role of the DC in dealing with institutional monies and estates of deceased persons in general. It is our recommendation that proper legal mandate be given to this office to mediate in this regard. This would provide for a forum, which is transparent, accountable and fair.

7.5   The criminalisation of dispossession of property of widows should fall under the realm of the proposed domestic violence law, and should specifically target the culprits of this offence who are usually the relatives of the deceased person.

7.6   In efforts to amend or repeal existing laws, government and NGOs must work together to share a common knowledge of diverse grounded experiences.

7.7   There is also need to examine the land law and the implications of matrilineality and patrilineality *Vis a Vis* the principles of equality.

7.8   The office of the District Assembly, being a central government office in all districts, is inundated with cases of dispossession of widows most of which it fails to effectively resolve because of incapacity, in terms of personnel and systems. There is therefore a need to empower the offices with adequate resources such as stationery or office equipment in order for staff to keep records and effectively conduct their affairs.

However the incapacity in terms of training and education of staff seriously hampers the ability to effectively deal with matters relating to dispute resolution, division of institutional monies and any other work relating to these offices.

Not only is there need for retraining of current staff, but there is also need to recruit staff who are better educated, who should then be trained in alternative dispute resolution methods.

7.9 Legal Rights Education for Women and Stakeholders

It is recommended that the civil society and government should institute intense awareness campaigns which should explain the nature, advantages and disadvantages of using the law as it relates to courts jurisdiction, and/or District Assemblies office's jurisdiction over estates of the deceased persons. Such campaigns would be more effective and informative, in the light of the present study.

Further such campaigns should relate to rights in marriages celebrated under the Marriage Act and customary law marriages.

There is need for awareness campaigns for the role of District Assemblies in storage of wills and also for the modalities in writing wills. This knowledge should be targeted at structures, men and women.

7.10 General Recommendations

In general, the research has shown that most people are not aware of their legal rights relating to Wills and Inheritance provisions. It is recommended therefore that there should be intense awareness campaigns which should explain the nature, advantages and disadvantages of the law as it relates to courts jurisdiction over deceased estates. Such campaigns would be very effective and informative, if they were based on the present research being conducted on the area.

Communities usually tolerate violence 'against women' that occurs in the form of dispossession of widows because it is considered a private matter. What is important is for the state, communities and individuals to assume responsibility for eliminating this type of gender-based violence.

What societies need are comprehensive approaches of civic education that involve human rights training in a series of workshops to assist widows to claim their rights. Women need to be empowered with knowledge and information as well as access to economic, social and political resources. In addition, there is need to reform

105

people's perceptions towards inheritance laws and practices through civic education.

7.11   It must be understood that legal reforms alone will not give an equitable advantage to a woman if the same is not complemented by economic and social change that ensure that women achieve equal material and legal capacity. National economic programmes must include women as a specific gender at formulation and implementation stage.

7.12   One of the fundamental problems facing the position of women in Malawi is a serious lack of networking among women's groups, government and stakeholders and the international community who together would properly collaborate on law reform and law enforcement. There is need therefore to create or strengthen such networks.

7.13   It was apparent among some widows interviewed, that there is lack of support from fellow women who are ordinarily the primary point of justice.[1] There is need therefore to strengthen networks among family, neighbours, and with women organizations and legal advice centres like WLSA, Women's Voice, Malawi CARER or CILIC is of central importance, both as a source of support and as means of intervention during processes of dispossession of widows.[2]

7.14   Although there is not a lot of research done to create a link between violence against women (especially its resistance) to education of women, some researchers have found that[3] women have been able to resist violence perpetrated against them if they had progressed beyond five years of formal education. This may be understood in the light of the fact that violence perpetrates fear. Levels of fear are determined by the amount of awareness that is contained in the subject of fear. The more educated women are, the less afraid they become and the more that they will take on perpetrators of property dispossession head on by invoking the formal and informal justice delivery system structures. It is recommended therefore that an increase in female education as that initiated by the Gable Project be put in place as well as strengthening of adult literacy programmes through the Ministry of Gender Youth and Community Services with special focus on women.

7.15   Although some cases indicated that employment or economic independence in itself did not preclude widows from dispossession, as a form of gender-based violence, it was clear that employment and other income generating bases would emerge as a foundation for starting over, once such property dispossession had taken place.

Therefore, the creation of jobs for women or income-generating activities at government policy making levels, would not only uplift women from a poverty state, it would also shield them from traumatic experiences that specifically happen to them by virtue of their sex, in this instance dispossession of widows.

7.16   Engendering the Budget

It appears that unequal distribution of resources in the justice delivery system structures has created problems for women and this has perpetuated inequality. Effective access to and control of resources by women, which includes access to equitable justice, is therefore fundamentally lacking. Lack of gendered justice delivery structures, perpetuates poverty for women, as they are unable to remove obstacles facing them which make them fail to achieve objectives that would remove them from such poverty. Engendering the national budget would help to mainstream gender in the overall government budget expenditure, which has different impacts on men and women. In order to promote the enjoyment of rights as per the Constitution as well as bring gender equality in very practical terms[4] engendering the budget would include, among other things, identifying gender-based expenditures of government departments and authorities; such as women's access to justice, training for clerical officers, as well as re-writing job descriptions to reflect equal employment opportunities.

7.17   Strategic gender lawyering would also be helpful. This will involve using the courts to change the law as well as attitudes relating to wrongs committed in inheritance matters especially in dispossession of widows. The principle of *ultra vires* in the Constitution would be the main guiding factor.

---

[1] WLSA Malawi,(2000)

[2] Sen, P, p.12

[3] ibid.

[4] White,(2000)

BIBLIOGRAPHY

Archakl Kapir," 1998: *A Profile of Saksi Violence* Oxfam Gender and Development Vol. 6 No. 3.

Alwan, S. V., 1997.*Review of NGO Activity in Zimbabwe Concerning Inheritance Rights of Widows and Orphans,* Save the Children Federation

Amadiume, I., (1987),, *Gender and Sex in an African Society,* Zed Books Ltd, London

Armstrong, A. K., 1998 *Culture and Choice- Lessons from Survivors of Gender Violence in Zimbabwe.* Harare, Zimbabwe,

Bentzon et A. W. et al, (1998): Pursuing Grounded Theory in Law: South –North Experiences in Developing Women's Law, Monde Books, Harare

Byrnes, 1992, "*Women Feminism and International Human Rights Law – Methodological, Fundamental Flaws or Meaningful Marginalisation*", Australian Yearbook, Vol. 12.

Chambers R. (ed) *Special Issues on "Vulnerability: How the Poor Cope,"* IDS Bulletin, Vol. 20, No 2

Chilambo and Jere, 1998 *MacMillan School Atlas,* Macmillan, Blantyre

Chizumila, T., 1998. *Widows Experiences,* unpublished article, paper presented at Wills and Inheritance Seminars in Mzuzu, Lilongwe and Mangochi

Connors, J., 1992, *Government Measures to Confront Violence Against Women*

Cook R. (ed.),, 1994.*Human Rights of Women- National and International Perspectives,* Philadelphia, University of Pennsylvania Press

Core Group on The Wills and Inheritance, 1998. *Proposal to Amend the Wills and Inheritance Act of Malawi,* unpublished report

Dow, U., and Kidd, P.,(1994): *Women Marriage and Inheritance,* WLSA Botswana, Botswana,

Elliot, F. R, 1996 *Gender, Family and Society*, Macmillan Press Ltd.

Griffith, J. (1986): "What is Legal Pluralism" in *Journal of Legal Pluralism and Unofficial Law*. Number 24

Hirschman, D, and Vaughan, M., 1983, *Food Production and Income Generation in Matrilineal Society: Rural Women in Zomba, Malawi*, in Journal of Southern Africa Studies, Vol. 10

Ibik J.O (1970), *Restatement of African Law Malawi*, The Law of Marriage and Divorce, Sweet and Maxwell, London.

Jimusole, T., 1997. *Gender Bias in Malawian Customary Family Law*, Unpublished dissertation,University Of Malawi

Kanyongolo, F., (July 2000) *Inequality and Dispossession of Widows and Children: A Framework for Analysis*, a paper presented at a Domestic Violence Seminar (unpublished), Blantyre, Malawi

Kasman E., and Chirwa,C,(1997), Integrated Food Security Programme, Mulanje

Mbiti J. S, (1987), " Flowers in the Garden – the Role of Women in African Religion, In the Place of African Traditional Religion in Contemporary Africa, Nairobi: Council for World Religion

Ncube and Stewart (Eds), (1995), *Widowhood, Inheritance Laws, Customs and Practices in Southern Africa: Regional Comparative Report on Inheritance*, WLSA, Zimbabwe.

Ncube W. and Stewart J (eds.). (1995) *Widowhood, Inheritance Laws, Customs and Practices in Southern Africa: Regional Comparative Report on Inheritance*, WLSA, Harare, Zimbabwe.

Nkhoma and Kirwan, (1996), *"Social Change and Widowhood: The Experience of the Tonga People of Malawi":* Unpublished Seminar Paper.

Owen,M. 1996:*A World of Widows*, London, Zed Books

Papadopoulos, N. 1998 *Reports of the Inheritance Workshop* held in Lobi, Chintheche and Namwera, Save the Children Federation, May.

Phiri I.A, (1997), *Women, Presbyterianism and Patriarchy, Religious Experiences of Chewa Women in Central Malawi*, A Kachere Monograph: Christian Literature Association of Malawi, Blantyre, Malawi

Phiri K.M, (1983), "Some Changes in The Matrilineal Family System Among The Chewa of Malawi Since The Nineteenth Century," in Journal of African History, Vol. 24,

Sakala F., (1998), "Violence Against Women in Southern Africa" in Southern Africa in Transition: A Gendered Perspective

109

Smith, P., (Ed.), 1993. *Feminist Jurisprudence*, New York: Oxford University Press,

Speech delivered by Honourable Samuel Kandodo Banda, then Chair of the Legal Affairs Committee of Parliament, at the launch of the White Scarf Campaign during the 16 days of Activism Against Violence Against Women, (25th November 2000).

Stewart J., et al, 1998 *Pursuing Grounded Theory in Law: South- North Experiences in Developing Women's Law*, Mond Books, Norway,

Tanamaha, B. Z, (1993): "The Folly of the Social Scientific Concept of Legal Pluralism" in *Journal of Law and Society*, Volume 20:3

Tang C. s. *et al* (2000): "*Exploring How the Chinese Define Violence Against Women: A Focus Group Discussion*" In Forum Vol. 1 No. 2, Pergamons

The Government Of Malawi (2000) The *1998 Malawi Population and Housing Census Report* by National Statistical Office, Zomba, Malawi.

UNDP Human Development Reports

UNICEF/GOM, (1997) Government of Malawi: *The National Platform for action , Follow up to the 4th World Conference in Women*, UNICEF/GOM

United nations / Government of Malawi, 1993, *Situation Analysis of Poverty in Malawi* Lilongwe, Malawi

United Nations, 1993, *Strategies for Confronting Domestic Violence: A Resource Manual*, New York, United Nations.

Walker, G. (1990): *Family Violence and the Women's Movement: The conceptual politics of Struggle,* University of Toronto Press. Toronto.

White, Seodi. 1998 *The Wills and Inheritance Act and The Wills and Inheritance Bill*, unpublished article, presented at Wills and Inheritance Seminars in Mzuzu, Lilongwe and Mangochi.

White, Seodi. 1998. *Wills and Inheritance (Amendment) Bill 1997: Justification and Need for Review*, unpublished article

Wing A (1997) *A Critical Race Conceptualization of Violence. South African and Palestinian Women.University of Pennsylvania*

WLSA Malawi (2000) *In Search of Justice, Women And The Administration Of Justice In Malawi,* Dzuka Publishing Company Limited, Blantyre, Malawi

WLSA Mozambique, (1996), *The Right to Succession and Inheritance*, Women and Law in Southern Africa Trust, Mozambique Maputo

WLSA Swaziland, (1998), *Family in Transition, The Experience of Swaziland*, Women and Law in Southern Africa Trust Swaziland Mbabane

WLSA Zambia (1994), *Inheritance in Zambia: Law and Practice*, WLSA, Lusaka Zambia

WLSA Zambia, (1997), *The Changing Family in Zambia*, Women and Law in Southern Africa Trust; Zambia Lusaka

WLSA Zimbabwe, *Paradigms of Exclusion: Women's Access to Resources in Zimbabwe (1997)*, WLSA Zimbabwe, Harare, Zimbabwe

WLSA, (1995) *Picking up the Pieces, Widowhood in Southern Africa* WLSA, Working Paper No. 213 Harare, Zimbabwe

APPENDIX

List of Statutes and Instruments

Convention on The Elimination Of All forms Discrimination Against Women, 1979

Government of Malawi, 1995 *The Constitution of the Republic of Malawi,* Government of Malawi,

Government of Malawi, *The Penal Code Cap* 7:01

Government of Malawi, *The Wills and Inheritance Act* Cap 10:02

SADC, *Declaration on Gender* by SADC, 1997

The Beijing Platform for Action, 1995.

The United Nations Declaration of Human Rights 1948

The Vienna Declaration of Human Rights, 1993

Printed in the United Kingdom
by Lightning Source UK Ltd.
108291UKS00001B/272